THE MAN WHO SANG
YELLOW SUBMARINE
IN LATIN

DEREK ENRIGHT
1935-1995

EDITORS
BRIAN LEWIS, JANE ENRIGHT
DUNCAN ENRIGHT & SIMON ENRIGHT

P

PONTEFRACT PRESS
1996

Published by:
Pontefract Press, 17 Linden Terrace, Pontefract, WF8 4AE

© Text: the contributors
© Photographs: the owners

Editorial Support:
Mandy Dandy, Reini Schühle, Jackie Enright,
Sally-Ann Enright, Judith Crooks and Tony Lumb

Cover Design:
Alan Studholme

Printed by:
FM Repro, Roberttown, Liversedge

ISBN: 1 900325 03 9

I was shocked to hear the news of Derek's death as I stood in traffic on the M25 last week. No doubt like me countless others whose lives he touched, scattered throughout the country, reflected on how far they had come and his role in their lives.

He underlined for me that I should not settle for less than I was capable of achieving.

Jane Horne

Introduction

The Requiem Mass for the repose of Derek's soul took place at Westminster Cathedral. It was a grand affair. Half of the Shadow Cabinet were there, as well as a sprinkling of Conservatives and a lot of Pontefract and District people who had travelled the two hundred miles to recall this modest, dignified man. The officiating priest, an old pupil of Derek's, told how he would have them translating The Guardian leaders into Ciceronian Latin before the school day began and the Deputy Speaker of the House of Commons, in a eulogy listing his civic achievements, told a story about him picking daffodils.

As we stood on the steps people came to the conclusion that the best way to remember Derek was quickly to publish a book so that two months after his death people who only knew part of his story would be able to celebrate his life with those who knew a bit more. That night a deadline was set. It was a tight one. The decision to write was made on 6 November, the deadline for contributions was three weeks later. As you can see, a lot of people responded quickly. We have tried to include something from everyone who sent us pieces.

We intended to list all the people who sent tributes in one form or another, but the task overwhelmed us. Well-wishers are still sending letters – over 900 at the last count – people are telephoning and stopping us in the street. We would just like to thank you all; your love and kindness has been a great support and it is a great comfort to know that so many people he knew feel his loss so keenly. That is the greatest epitaph anyone could ask for.

The Editors

Thornaby to Nevison

After Derek was born I stayed in bed running a temperature and feeling awful. My sister Winnie agreed to be godmother, and following tradition at the time took Derek off to be christened two days after his birth. She came back a little flustered. "Is Dominic the Latin for Derek?" she asked.

"No, Dominic is a completely different name," I replied, wondering what on earth she was on about.

"Oh dear, I think he has been christened the wrong name!" she cried.

I wasn't sure whether to believe her or not until the following Sunday, when I got the Parish magazine, and sure enough the baptism of 'Dominic Enright' was announced.

Dominic was the wrong name, I didn't like it, and so I wanted it put right straight away. I went to the priest who had christened him and had a right go at him. "Is my name Paleski?" I demanded. No of course it wasn't he murmured meekly. "If my name isn't Paleski, then my son isn't called Dominic. Sort it out" I said.

He did. I was glad, although Derek complained later that he rather liked the name Dominic!

Helen Enright

Born in Thornaby of Irish and Scottish stock, Derek was amongst the first of his generation of Catholic and other working-class children to benefit from the 1944 Education Act. He was the son of a railwayman victimised in the General Strike, and a mother who led a strike at a Pontefract liquorice factory.

He was brought up in the Lake District and, after the War, in Pontefract, with his two sisters Margaret and Helen. After St Joseph's School, Pontefract, and St Michael's College, Leeds,

Derek read Greats at Wadham College, Oxford University, before going to London to begin his career in teaching.

Duncan Enright

When Derek was a boy we lived at Gaisgill Railway Station House, in the Lake District. At the age of about four, he made a blunder that cost me a friend and the best pork pies I have ever tasted.

Our garden got very sloppy and muddy in the winter, and Derek liked to play outside in his boots. All day long he trailed in and out making the carpet filthy, despite all pleas. Eventually I pulled him up. "Will you wipe your feet when you come in. I'm sick of telling you!" Chastened he sat in the corner of the room.

A nearby farmer's wife kept pigs, and we had become friends. She had got into the habit of calling round with gifts of pork pies she made herself, the most delicious huge things the like of which I have never tasted before or since. She and her pies had always been welcome in our home.

That day she came round with a lovely great pork pie. Smiling she moved to put it down on the table. No sooner had she stepped into the room than a little voice piped up from the corner: "Will you wipe your feet when you come in. We're sick of telling you!"

She put down the pie with a grim look on her face, turned, and left without a word. I spoke to her many times after that, but she never entered our house again and that was the last pork pie she ever brought!

Helen Enright

He was my elder by a couple of years only so Derek and I always shared a family birthday party. As his birthday was in the summer holidays and mine in February these joint parties were always on my birthday. This meant that his friends felt obliged to give me a present but my friends didn't give him anything. Also we came out best in the party games - especially Postman's Knock! I can't understand why he was less than happy with this arrangement!

Margaret Hampson

I remember as a child of about ten, being chased around the garden of our Pontefract home while Derek practised a new found skill of lassooing. He was quite good at this and many times caught me and my friend, Patricia, with his rope.

Helen Boggett

When we were about eight years old at St. Joseph's School, Pontefract, we began serving at mass and so had to learn the Latin responses. Derek, even at that age, picked it up quickly. Derek's father, a wonderful man who unfortunately died in his late fifties, and mother, soon taught Derek a deep love of his faith and socialism. We served together at Knottingley in what he called the Conservative rooms and as an eight year old I can remember him standing on a chair to turn the pictures to the wall. He took great delight in doing it to Winston Churchill's.

We went to St Michael's together, where he was an outstanding student, and at about fifteen he was allowed by the College to go down to the Leeds town hall steps and do some soap box speaking for the Young Christian Workers. He had to have a license to do that and I believe he was the youngest person to get one. His love of Yorkshire cricket started at about twelve when after school we would race over to Headingley to try to catch the last couple of hours. If we managed to see Len Hutton, later of course Sir Len, batting, it made our day. As teenagers we played tennis at our local welfare where we spent many happy days and although neither of us were very good, neither of us liked losing.

Ray Valente

Happy memories of childhood are evoked whenever I think of Derek. Known by the highly original name of 'Duckleft', he was one of our 'gang'. We all pretended to play tennis, emulating the great tennis aces: Hoad, Rosewall, etc. in the 1950's at the Townville Welfare – known as the 'Rec'. We would congregate, mostly on the wall of number 31 Sheepwalk Lane, where we would put the world to rights, to the annoyance of the neighbours.

Even in the early days Derek was always destined to do great things. He had a wonderful intellect but I think was rather lacking in sparring partners from our group. I learned, at an early age, never to enter into a political discussion with Derek or annihilation would surely follow. The situation at that time was rather volatile as my father was Chairman of Castleford Conservative Club and Derek was always eager for a conversion, the more challenging the better. However, they were to become great friends for the rest of my father's life.

The boring bus journey to Leeds and back every day was undertaken by the pupils from St Michael's, Notre Dame and Mount St. Mary's in those days. The twenty past four bus from Leeds Bus Station to Pontefract and Castleford was the highlight of the day and was considerably enhanced when Derek was on the bus. He had quite a repertoire of jokes, you know the kind that go on for ever? I can still remember the punch line of his 'Rary-Bird' joke which was 'It's a long way to Tip-a-Rary'.

In later years he taught my children, instilling in them a true interest in the subject studied, the essential requirement of a good teacher and achieved fantastic results, assisting them in a good start in this world. How wonderful it was to know that he represented us in 'The House'. I would find myself looking for him on the television and proudly say 'That's Derek there'! I like to think that he continues to represent us in Heaven.

Margaret Valente

Our father had a faith to move mountains. His belief in God, and the Roman Catholic faith, was always an ingredient of what he did and said. It was of course partly through the church that he received his education, although it was very much his family that set the tone of his beliefs, which involved a steadfast adherence to the church and a liberal interpretation of its teachings.

As a young man while still at school, he carried a soapbox around Leeds in the late 1940s and early 1950s preaching for the Young Christian Workers. He was the youngest to receive the licence to speak in public. He described one useful ploy for drawing a crowd, which contributed to his success.

People seldom stop to hear a street speaker, as many know to their cost or find out in gruelling and often embarrassing election campaigns. But by the age of fifteen or so, the young Derek has developed a foolproof crowd-pulling scam.

Standing on top of his orange box, on a Leeds shopping street corner in the grey afternoon after drizzle, he draws from his pocket a brightly coloured yo-yo. A couple stop and stare. Deliberately plucking the string to its full extent and slowly winding it around the bobbin, he prepares the toy for action. Another man stops, and two people leaning against the wall begin to take notice. With cracking wrist and a swoosh of the sleeve, he sets the yo-yo going, skimming along its line to a whirring halt at its low point, skidding like a cartoon character on the turn, then letting it curl up again and nestle against his palm.

More and more people in heavy damp coats slow their step and gaze at the daft young lad on the box with a yo-yo. Sometimes the yo-yo snags, and wheels helplessly like a Sopwith Camel hit by enemy fire. Derek patiently untangles the thread and sets it going again, up and down, smooth and spinning. With intense concentration he seems to frown at the effort. Grimly he stoops over the whirring bobbin, feigning ignorance of the gathering folk on the pavement. When enough people stop, others stop to see what they are looking at. Soon a regular crowd is peering at the disc as it rises and falls. Unconsciously their breath takes pace from the yo-yo, and up and down go the chests of the coats of the people wondering why the dark-haired young eejit on the crate is playing silly beggars on a Saturday on the Headrow.

Without looking up from the yo-yo, Derek begins to speak. Clear and loud, though not projected, for his face is still pointing at the undulating bobbin with which his words keep time, his voice carries out into the crowd who hush to hear: "Life... is... like... a... YO-YO!"; and at that word he snatches the toy from its trajectory and stands erect.

"It has its ups and downs!" he declaims, and to the startled shuffle of Leeds shoppers caught unawares he begins to preach and teach the Good News of the Lord, who holds the string on which we bob and glide.

Duncan Enright

Oxford to London

Among the sixty or so young men who applied to read Classics at Wadham in January 1953 Derek Enright, from St Michael's, Leeds, did not stand out as a sparkling star in Latin, still less in Greek. But he stood out well enough in impish intelligence to be one of the eight chosen by Maurice Bowra and his fellow examiners. He went on to justify the choice, not in academic achievement but in the life he gave to the tutorial, to the quad, the JCR (and Bar), with, of course, Maurice Howse's pantry as a last retreat.

Derek was a man of contradictions. I mention three. No one could pretend that he devoted himself to his studies – the bright remarks that he made tutorially (and there were many very bright and very percipient remarks) reflected a background of glorious idleness or absorption in other things. Yet he loved the Classics with a real passion that he carried on into his teaching. First he was at the John Fisher School, Purley, to which he attracted two other Wadham contemporaries, Michael Dunworth and Noel Worswick, and with them created a powerful and enlightened Classical team. Then he moved to North Featherstone. Within four years, from a brand new comprehensive school, he was sending candidates to Oxford and Cambridge in Classics; in the late sixties, some achievement. After that it came as no surprise, even a bit of an anti-climax, that he should address the House of Commons in Latin. "Why not Greek?", I asked him. "Bit rusty", he replied, cool as ever under tutor's fire.

There, in the House as MP for Hemsworth from 1991, we see the result of another contradiction or, rather, ambivalence. Derek came up in 1954 as a Socialist from a staunch Socialist family and, within the College (he never showed any ambition to be a University politician) he stuck to his Socialist guns, even as President of the JCR. But he was also a Catholic who loved his church as deeply as he loved his Classics. Thus there was, in some areas, a pull to the right which drew him over the years from mild support for Aneurin Bevan to warm adherence to Tony Blair.

The last contradiction is superficial. Late one night (say 4am) undergraduate Derek leant forward, forearms across thighs, one admonishing finger raised (friends will remember the pose) and said, in that best Yorkshire accent which he could assume for such moments, "This place should be abolished; it's socially oonjoost." There spoke the actor. He did not mean it and I was not surprised when his older son, Duncan, followed his father as undergraduate and then as President of the JCR at Wadham, that unjust place.

There could be no more loyal or likeable member of the College. Old members will recall his presence at Gaudies and Society parties (including one which he organised in the House of Commons). They will also recall the grin and the touch of irresponsible fun which made him such an agreeable pupil.

George Forrest

I remember a great long weekend spent with my brother in his days at Oxford. He took me to the theatre to see a Gilbert and Sullivan production, and to a ball, providing both an escort and an orchid, although I was much more impressed by the orchid than the escort!

After another evening out in the hostelries of Oxford we returned to his room in Wadham to play Poker. As it was late and women were not allowed in we had to get in by climbing over a barbed wire fence, on which I cut my foot, and then over a wall which had a manure heap next to it – most convenient for the ladies and the gentleman from our party with a broken foot!

The next night was our last and we had to catch an early morning train, so it hardly seemed worth paying for another night's B+B. We also had to continue the Poker game. But where? We couldn't risk climbing into College again so we 'borrowed' a boat and rowed over to Wadham's barge. In those days each Oxford college owned a barge on the river which was used as a boathouse. We finished the game there!

As Derek saw me off on the train he confided that he had told his friends that it would be a quiet weekend! I finished up having to get a tetanus jab a couple of days later but it was well worth it!

Margaret Hampson

We hosted his 21st Birthday Party in Pontefract. Many friends of the family were there and drink was flowing freely. We hadn't decided what to get him and hadn't really got many ideas either.

Somebody at the party asked him what he wanted as he was fetching a drink and he replied casually over his shoulder "Kim Novak". His father Laurie took me on one side and asked quietly how much a Kim Novak would cost, thinking it was a make of camera! At least we all got a good laugh even if Derek didn't get his Kim!

Helen Enright

Although I had an uncle in Leeds, as a London boy born and partly bred, I knew very few Yorkshiremen. I was a southerner so when I visited Derek at his family home in Pontefract on my first long vacation from Oxford I discovered the fine warmth of a Yorkshire working class community. It was at this time, I suppose, that I became aware of the real culture of the other half of the country I lived in. Derek was a great convivial singer and his repertoire included what were then known as Irish Rebel songs. I have never forgotten the songs we sang as students and I have never forgotten their (political) meaning. But most of all I remember Derek's astonishing ability to make a coherent whole of his background in Pontefract and his Classical education.

Derek introduced me to the reality of working class culture –

which is the equal of any other culture, and totally authentic. Thank you Derek for your warmth, humanity, and for introducing me to Yorkshire, where I made my home.

Roland Miller

At College Derek made the most of family connections. His father was Station Master at Ferrybridge and his mother at that time worked in a launderette. He would bundle his dirty clothes onto the train at Oxford station, and receive a pristine parcel of clean and pressed clothes on the express the following day.

Duncan Enright

St John's Wood is a long way from Camberwell. It was well away from my normal area of partying in South Ken and Chelsea, but I was flattered by the invitation to join my work colleagues Margaret and Joanna at their flat-warming and intrigued by the advance publicity of the guests who were to include some of Joanna's brother's friends from Oxford. So determining to leave the party by 11pm to join friends in Chelsea, I set out on the long ride south over the river to De Crespigny Park in Camberwell.

The friends were nice, particularly the smaller and noisier of the two who arrived in a disreputable old navy gabardine raincoat belted round the waist like a schoolboy. It turned out Derek was inordinately fond of this garment which was to play a disproportionately large part in our early courtship as it had to be rescued from pubs and clubs all over London where it was left hanging innocently on a peg. It just wasn't the sort of garment that people stole and it always managed to turn up just where it had been left with its full complement of handkerchiefs, match boxes and bus tickets in its pockets. It probably still hangs somewhere as after about eight months of galloping across Town to retrieve it, finally we forgot where we had been the night before and the mac was abandoned to a solitary life of dust gathering until such time as the landlord saw fit to throw it out or give it to a good cause.

My 11 o'clock deadline passed and we continued to sing and laugh until the small hours when Derek, gallant but unwise, offered to take me home in a taxi. Off we set across sleeping London. We promised to meet the following evening at 7.30 at London Bridge station and then Derek set off back the way he had come. He only had money enough to get halfway home himself that night and had to walk the last three miles or so.

In some trepidation I set out on the following evening for London Bridge and there I waited in mounting rage for half an hour before starting home, swearing never again to speak to Yorkshiremen in gabardine raincoats.

Derek rang me in my office the following morning, and every morning after, abject with apologies. He had finally arrived home with the morning papers, and had fallen asleep at lunchtime only to wake at 7.30pm. He set out to London Bridge to find me gone.

After the bombardment of phone calls my obduracy finally softened somewhat and I agreed to meet him again after 10 days. Chastened and neatly belted into the gabardine, Derek met me in Fleet Street and gave me a sweet smelling white freesia in a little paper bag. Together we went to the pictures and saw Les Enfants du Paradis at which we both wept inconsolably. As we stumbled out to the street I found that I had been carrying my paper bag upside down and my beautiful freesia had fallen out somewhere to be trampled underfoot - but it didn't matter! It was the beginning of a beautiful friendship.

Jane Enright

Derek's flat was always a mess, but I remember with particular horror visiting one day to find gunge soaking in the sink. "How old is this tripe?" I asked, only to be told it was socks, halfway through being washed.

Helen Enright

When Derek first started teaching in Purley, he lived in a rather bleak large flat in Penge. This he shared with Warren Stevenson, a friend from Wadham, and for a while with Charlie Pass, a friend of Warren's from Bolton. One of the bedrooms in the flat was sublet to a married couple but no-one seemed to know who they were or when they came and went – possibly they are living there still.

Warren and Derek lived exclusively on meat pies and beer sold by the pub at the top of the road, called The Railway. Much jollification was to be had at The Railway but the meat pies were not to be recommended except to those of the strongest constitution.

Times were hard and money became shorter still when, during that first summer, Charlie Pass, a somewhat flash fellow, suddenly disappeared back North with the rent and the rental for the television hire that Derek and Warren had been paying him. He was not heard of for many years until he turned up, an extremely respectable citizen, as Chief Education Officer for a Lancashire town! He never refunded his 'borrowing' of the rent money!

Jane Enright

John Fisher to St Wilfrid's

The John Fisher School in Purley when Derek started teaching there in 1959, was an impressive day school for boys with a splendid entrance, chapel and cricket field and school buildings which was backed by various houses in the vicinity.

A rather haphazard regime existed in the school under the eccentric guidance of the Headmaster, the doughty Canon. The many priests who helped to staff the school were wished upon him by the Bishop who would often place them there after they had become ill in their Parishes in order that they could have "a rest". This is the only time in my experience that I have ever heard of teaching prescribed as a rest cure! The lay staff were, however, hand picked by the Head and the whole unlikely mixture worked amazingly well with magnificent results being achieved by many of the boys who clamoured to come to the school from the whole of Surrey and South London.

Wages at the time that Derek started at the Fisher were comparatively low. Along with the rest of the impecunious laymen on the staff, he would go to the Canon if particularly broke to ask if he could delay paying tax at the end of a month when he found himself particularly hard up. This system, satisfactory to all, was discovered by the Inland Revenue one appalling Summer. They put into the school a special Tax Adviser who with infinite patience and ingenuity tried to sort out the school's affairs. Derek was never again allowed to hold over his tax, but he was granted several allowances as the poor Tax Adviser tried to tackle the inconsistencies and vagaries of the previous system.

When Derek after just a year was appointed Head of Classics, he was the first lay Head of Department in the history of the school.

Jane Enright

Derek's sixth form Religious Education lessons had all the informality of the classic Oxford tutorial. Once in 1972 a small group of us were gathered in his study discussing the moral teaching of a recent Papal encyclical, whilst Derek, his feet resting on the corner of his desk, was puffing away at one of his black cheroots. A small cloud of smoke hung lazily in the air. Suddenly an urgent knock on the door was followed by a member of staff who announced that two boys had been found smoking around the back of the gym'.

Derek's demeanour instantly changed to one of shock and disbelief. "Smoking? Smoking!" he boomed in his best baritone voice. Swinging his legs from the desk and placing the cheroot in the ashtray in the same fluid movement, he swept out of the room like an avenging angel.

Those of us remaining in the room could only imagine the scene of carnage in the corridor outside from the verbal barrage which was being inflicted upon the two miscreants:

"Smoking! Smoking in School! Smoking in a Catholic school!"

How could the stoop so low? How could they inflict such shame and disgrace upon their families? Their poor mothers! How could they hope to achieve anything worthwhile with their lives if they had already reached such a sad state of moral decline?

Then, as swiftly as the onslaught had begun, it ended. Derek dismissed the two unfortunates to do their penance, having left them in no doubt as to what would befall them if they ever were to think about indulging in such unnatural practices again.

Moments later he swept back into the room, tossed a battered packet of Woodbines into his desk drawer and sat down. "Now, let that be a lesson to you all!" he said, as he carefully relit the cheroot.

Martin Hyde

I was a pupil at St Wilfrid's between 1970 and 1977 before going to Leeds University to study Classics. I recall my first few Latin lessons. The concoctions of nouns and verbs which I managed to produce bore little resemblance to Latin but, within a month, I had been securely fixed on my journey through the riches of the Classical world. From being totally puzzled by even the simplest syntax and conjugation of amo, amas, amat, I suddenly rose to the dizzy heights of joint top of the class with 98% or 100% scores.

Most O-level students however remained anti-Latin and, not wishing to incur the energetic Enright wrath, persuaded me to take on a lucrative homework contract paid for in chocolate bars and ice pops.

Soon I had achieved a clientele of about six and was putting on weight. However, after about three months the January exams loomed and, as all deceivers are found out, therein lay our downfall. I maintained my record but my 'disciples' managed to achieve less than 10% each!

The inquest followed and needless to say my chocolate rations disintegrated. I remember Derek saying that one day I would realize the effect of my, or our, deception.

As I approached my A-levels I was very unsure of what to do and Derek gave me the opportunity I needed. I couldn't choose between the sciences which I enjoyed and the Classics which I could handle well. Derek, although not on offer according to the list we had been given, kindly offered to allow me to do Ancient Greek with him as tutor and myself sole pupil. I could, at some point in the following two years, choose to continue or drop subjects. He had given me time to make my mind up, given me time and encouragement.

Steve Bontoft

Since I left school over eighteen years ago, I have worked in more than a dozen countries and visited many more. Whilst work is interesting, the constant travel and change plays havoc with one's memories. People once met in government offices turn up as refugees, friends living in areas of conflict are killed, others die of Aids. Hundreds of other people met in meetings, offices, conferences, villages, towns and refugee and displaced camps fade into oblivion brought to the surface by a photograph or another's memories. Yet some memories never fade.

It was Mr Enright to me as a child, Derek to my parents, who taught me Greek at school. I learnt Greek out of school hours. He must have been mad to give up his time. I really benefited. He had a passion for Greek which was a pleasure to listen to. The language was no longer dead but full of life and vitality. I am reminded of him when I listen to Somalis reciting poetry who share the same pleasure in not only the story but the words and the rhythm of the language.

Other memories are vaguer: a trip to Guinea Bissau, hot and steamy, a drive through tropical forest, crossing a ferry, birds in a glassed off room, gin and tonics before lunch – refreshingly cool in the humid climate, stories of the independence struggle, the Portuguese looting the country down to the last typewriter as they left, diplomatic multi-lingual dinners, hand-rolled cigarettes with liquorice paper, a wine-tasting session, school musicals – Gilbert and Sullivan and black gowns, pub lunches, family get-togethers and baby sitting.

Jane Macaskill

As my Head of Sixth Form Derek helped set the course for most of my life. His example of not shirking difficult decisions, maintaining high standards, being charitable when forming opinions and above all caring for people, had a real effect on those young people in his charge.

It was Derek who offered me two terms of temporary employment which seventeen years later I have yet to complete. It was a privilege, not only to work alongside him, but also to teach most of his family. His leaving to become an MEP is still vaguely remembered by all those who were there to assist in his personal solution to the wine lake problem.

Each visit to school was a welcome opportunity to greet him. He played an influential role on all our lives. He took great inspiration from the words of the hymn "To be a pilgrim". We may have smiled in 1972 but that advice has served us well.

David Bellwood

St Wilfrid's RC High School, Featherstone, was a tough school, but Derek Enright was a tough man: not in the physical sense (although he delivered robust chastisement to those who consciously breached the high standard of discipline) but in that it's always a battle to maintain the highest standards of Christian life. This he did amongst nearly 2000 children for many years, drawn from the prosperous and boisterous mining villages.

As a Latin teacher he fostered a love of, and respect for, the Classics and I developed life-long skills under his tutelage. I will remember and mourn Derek Enright because he enabled me to become the person that I am; proud of St Wilfrid's Latin motto: Fidem Servavi, St Paul's boast "I have kept the Faith"; loving study for its own sake; with a sense of duty and service and pride in my county, my country and my people's traditions.

Look at the Latin derivation of English words - a pursuit highly recommended by Derek. The root of 'Education' is Educere: 'to lead out'. Well, he led us all out into the world as proud bearers of Christ's message and hungry for truth and justice.

Mark Wilson

```
PONTEFRACT & CASTLEFORD LOCAL GROUP C.S.E.

                          St. Wilfrid's R C High
                                    School,
                          Cutsyke Road,
                              N. Fe the sto e

                          Po tefr:   2096 or 72228


Dear Cha rm   or Sec  t ry,

      At the Loc 1 Gr oup m eting it  s decided th t the
Ch irm   nd Secre  -y of the Loc 1 G  oup should hold
meeting with the Ch irme  nd Secr t   e of subj ct
p els   I h ve be   ble to fi d   d te for the me ti g
t t he Flying Horse, P tefr  ct on Thursd y, th October
t 7.30.  If for ny re so you re u ble to tte d, I
would be gr teful if you would  re ge for  substitute.

      The I iti  Agreement Tri l ill t ke nl e c Frid y,
24th Oct ober  t St. Wilfrid's from 9.15  m.

                    Yours sincer ely,

                    [signature]

                    D. A  E right
                    Loc 1 G oup Sec   t ry
```

I am enclosing a photocopy of a letter Derek sent to me regarding a CSE meeting in September 1975. He was Group Organiser for every subject and I was Head of Geography at St Wilfrid's and a CSE District Secretary for the subject.

Upon receipt of this fabulous script I went to see him for a translation and he apologised for the typewriter saying:

(i) it had lain in the loft for a long time and the bats and the pigeons had shit on it

(ii) on being carried downstairs it had been dropped, and bounced down several stairs – he said the cat caught it and it broke its tail and its back leg

(iii) what was I complaining about, it still typed English and not Chinese.

Bill Briggs

At St Wilfrids topics under discussion ranged from the most fundamental questions regarding man's existence to the most inconsequential trifle imaginable. We even talked about education sometimes. It mattered little to Derek; he could discourse with equal facility on Dostoyevsky's "Great Furnace of Doubts" or the mistackle that had let in the Widnes centre for the match winning try the previous Saturday. He excelled, of course, when political issues were on the agenda and, with a subtle mixture of genuine conviction, low cunning and a few apposite, if bogus, statistics would gleefully wind up the handful of Tories present (in those days, incredible as it may seem, there were two or three in most schools). The amazing thing was that they loved him for it and kept coming back for more. It takes a rare talent to be able to say things people don't want to hear in such a way that they enjoy the experience.

The highlight of the week, however, was Thursday evening when this happy band stayed at school after lessons, ostensibly to supervise pupils doing homework. This institution was optimistically known as "Evening Study". The fact of the matter was that there were invariably more teachers than students around because the real point of the evening was not only, as school policy implied, to provide a comfortable working environment for pupils with difficult home conditions, but to give this coterie a good excuse for prolonging its activities, first of all in school and, after opening time, in the Bradley Arms. At the beginning of each academic year, Derek, religiously and inevitably, booked himself in for the Thursday evening to supervise the supervisors.

It was on one of these evenings, I think, that, apart from his other attributes, I really became aware of Derek's true quality as a teacher. An extra class had been organised for an A-level Latin group and, having little else to do (probably because there was no one to supervise) I and a few other redundant colleagues decided to go along, even though the subject matter, the poetry of

Catullus, was unknown territory for all of us. The decision turned out to be a good one. It was one of the best classes I ever attended. Derek spoke eloquently and knowledgeably for an hour and, as the cliche goes, had us in the palm of his hand. Laced with humour and illuminated by perceptive analysis it was a talk that had everything; this was no "Yellow Submarine" in Latin. Apart from anything else, skilfully constructed as it was, and expertly delivered, it was a lesson in how to teach.

John Clayton

There were many aspects of Derek's character that were admirable, but one of his most endearing qualities was an almost total lack of embarrassment. Whatever the circumstances, I cannot remember him being stuck for words, put off his stride, or even falter in his argument. He could use the most outrageous hyperbole without a blush, change tack without detection and above all, display his legendary grasp of statistics to trump any opponent's challenge.

Once when the Headmaster suggested to Derek that the Sixth Form were not working hard enough. Derek said that he found that very difficult to believe since 92.3% of the boys and 96.1% of the girls did more than three hours homework each night!

Very few of Derek's colleagues could produce such devastating statistics so quickly. But Derek could, and with a straight face! Of course, any man who could think of translating 'Yellow Submarine' into Latin and then have the cheek to deliver it to the House of Commons did not embarrass easily. And yet, there was nothing undignified about Derek. He was simply not pompous or pretentious but full of charm and sincerity.

Alan Whitehall

After Evening Study, it was doubtless to the Bradley Arms we went to end the evening with the customary blend of darts, dominoes and debate. Derek's stated preference was always for dominoes though goodness knows why, given the difficulty he experienced sorting out numbers between one and six, especially when it came to beer. The occasional inexactitude or selective amnesia which characterised his way with statistics would also affect him when it came to adding up the pints consumed.

"Are we off then, Derek?"

"We'll just have one more."

"We've had four already." (a figure endorsed by all present minus one)

"Nonsense, I make it two and a half. Right, Who wants what then?"

And yet again he had the last word.

Jack Clayton

Derek was dedicated and infectiously enthusiastic in all his endeavours, at first in his teaching and then in political life. In the former he had a fascination for Classics which swept across a broad canvas, from Ancient Greek to Latin, from Greek and Roman History to Literature and Philosophy. In the latter his interests were equally diverse, from the needs of his constituents to the problems of the Third World, from women's rights to educational matters. He coupled these pursuits with the skills of polished communication, teaching, writing and speaking with an elegant finesse belying hours of meticulous study (the curiosa felicitas of Horace).

But also, just as importantly, he had the common touch. He responded to people and they were responsive to him. He cared about people and their problems whatever their backgrounds. This concern for others, coming as it did from a deep and enduring commitment to his Faith, was the bedrock of his educational and political philosophies.

But Derek was much more than the sum of his philosophies. He was a great family man. He was devoted to Jane and his children and from them, in return, enjoyed great support and drew strength. He was also much more than just a serious, scholarly person. His dedication, care and commitment were leavened by a keen, at times almost impish, sense of humour well seasoned with wit. Derek was very good company.

Mick Young

In the school office we were rather fond of having a drink, often in celebration for one reason or another, but often because we felt like one. One day we were caught in the act by Derek. "Now then, why are you lot drinking? There's nothing to celebrate today" he said disapprovingly. Quick as a flash I remembered something I had heard on the radio coming in that morning. "It's Trafalgar Day and we're having a drink for that," I said. "Well, in that case, you had better pour me one," he said, grinning.

Nora Finn

One Saturday morning, to the Flying Horse with my two sons after a swim. Three pints ordered. See Derek and join him. He greets us affably, but chokes his pint down and departs rapidly. Younger son suggests that the Deputy Head prefers not to be seen in public drinking with fourth and fifth year students. Tact is not my strong point.

Malcolm Macaskill

Pontefract to Wakefield

I always remember when I told Derek that I spent hours quoting Shakespeare to Maria as a small baby in the hope that something of his greatness might be inherited, he told me that he had quoted Latin to his own children when young with the same hope.

Mary Flemmington

The Enright family lived down the road from us and if I have to conjure them I see them twenty years ago not as I see them now. Derek is about forty. He is clean shaven, small boned, in a suit with a waistcoat. The waistcoat is plum-coloured. Jane is in tweeds, beautiful and walking the dog. Jane's dogs to my taste are rather ugly but she knows them to be beautiful though flat-faced and barrel-chested. Duncan is in a blazer, studious and quiet, Mandy is also quiet but smiles a lot, Jackie is more willowy with unruly hair and, tagged onto the end, is little Simon.

I do not see the rubicund patriarch or Jane, Justice of the Peace and caring administrator. Duncan is eleven years old and not a father and publisher with an Oxford firm and a difficult seat to win in Henley at the next election. Mandy isn't married or doing social work in Manchester or Jackie running swish restaurants in the City of London. Simon isn't the bulky man of television with a reading voice which would make Ian Paisley quake. How can they be. It's Christmas 1975 and Reini and I are taking a meal with them in Carleton Road.

Brian Lewis

I had given up on smoking several years before Derek and Jane came to Pontefract in 1967 (I sold the house to them in Carleton Road and instantly became a warm friend). Intrigued more by the liquorice paper than the filling and the method of production I was persuaded to try one. I did and I still have instant recall on how it tasted! Distinctly different, needing many matches to keep it alight.

As for those pints of ale, I marvelled for years how Derek was able to down so many. We planned to compile a book about Pontefract's pubs – something quite racy and but readable. Alas! It never came about despite often further promised avowals of interest.

Derek was also a founder member of the Civic Trust in 1969, and for a short while acted as Treasurer. I've typed up some of the early minutes and there, in the very first of them reporting the "Meeting held on 28 February 1969 to discuss the formation of a Civic Trust in Pontefract", the penultimate paragraph recorded: "The meeting appointed D. Enright to act as Treasurer and he immediately responded by collecting 5/- (five shillings) subscriptions from all present". Now that was Derek – no messing about, immediate decisive action! Would that he and I, later on, had been similarly decisive about the thing on Ponte's pubs!

Allan Blaza

We first met Derek, Jane and their two elder children nearly thirty years ago. It was an instant warmth. We knew Pontefract would be more fun with this young lively family in our midst. Derek and I found we had a lot in common, cradle Catholics and cradle Socialists. I worked with him in our local Labour Party. He was an enthusiastic worker, unselfish and sincere. Everyone who met Derek at that time became enthused by his youth and hard work. We lived and breathed politics. There were days when we had disappointments; Derek lost to the Conservatives once. He wouldn't let us down by showing how much he was hurt. Into the fray we went immediately.

I remember Pontefract and District Labour Party conducting a survey in a poor area of our town. We wanted to know how we could help. Jane and I knocked on doors, talking to everyone. I discovered a proud, lonely old lady who lived on her own in abject poverty. She refused our help and I knew with winter approaching how she would suffer. On my way home I called on Derek and told him how worried we were. Within a month he had a Social Worker for her and a heating allowance. This was the essence of Derek Enright. He cared about the weak and the vulnerable.

Perhaps our happiest memories were our Christmas eves together. The Enright family and their friends arrived. Our house had buzzed all afternoon preparing mince pies, festive drinks, presents for the children. Neighbours were invited to hear the children sing carols and ring their hand bells. It was pure happiness. Derek always made sure there was a collection for the needy.

Anne Mitchell

Frequent visits and constant concern for Yorkshire Cricket, Featherstone Rovers Rugby League, Frickley and Leeds United (or Middlesboro or Darlington or Hartlepool) Football Clubs punctuated Daddy's life. He shrank from accepting VIP status at matches on the few occasions he was offered it, unless invited specifically by a friend like Phil Edmonds at a Test Match at Headingley or Len Barraclough at Post Office Road.

On one occasion, when Daddy was the local MP, we went to Post Office Road to watch Featherstone against Castleford (unfortunately Cas won). On the way walking the half mile into the ground many people stopped us to say hello. Rather than join the members in the bar we took our place in the stand and waited for the game to begin.

Daddy always had a loud voice, and when Featherstone were close to scoring it got much louder. Even in defeat Fev frequently look like the classy side they are, so this happened often during the first half. One of the members heard him and at half-time we were ushered into the VIP section. Daddy didn't want to offend the kind person who offered by refusing the elevation, so we moved to the 'better' seat. But Daddy had knew what I didn't, that we would have enjoyed the game as much if not more down where we were before!

When the call came to defend Rugby League, and Featherstone who were not chosen for the new Super League sponsored by Rupert Murdoch, Daddy was one of the first to rise to the defence of the game and the Club, appearing on local and national news.

There was a two-minute silence at Post Office Road in his honour when he died, after which Fev were unceremoniously trounced. As in life so in death...!

Duncan Enright

I was too young to understand what a Councillor really did when my father was elected to West Yorkshire County Council. For, as he would unfailingly point out, he was not a Councillor but a County Councillor.

In addition to this, I also gained the impression that as well as being a teacher, my father had taken on a new role as a builder. He told me that he had worked as a Navvy during his student summer holidays, so when people had said, sometimes in derision, "Your father was responsible for that bloody pedestrianisation in Pontefract" I automatically assumed it was him that had laid the stones. What further proof did I need than a photo of him, shovel in hand, planting the trees.

The main duty of a County Councillor, as it certainly seemed to me, was to participate in Cricket matches against Councillors from other Counties. It was most enjoyable to sit in the Seventies summer sun and watch my father play.

I remember his brave batting: he always seemed to be protecting his wicket after the early collapse of his colleagues. His bowling was medium pace to slow, but usually accurate. He often claimed to be a spinner but certainly never passed on this skill. Most memorable of all, however, was his fielding. He was slim, lithe and quick way into his late forties. He took quite a few boundary catches and rarely let a ball get past him in the field.

However, there was one occasion when a sturdy Doncaster fellow did get the better of him. Dad was in the outfield just near us and the ball, having past him, was heading for the boundary. I watched from a bench as it raced towards me with my father in valiant pursuit. The ball arrived first, striking me on the leg. My first reaction was shock and silence. I hadn't realised cricket balls were so hard.

Simon Enright

Every Sunday in summer as a child, I used to make Daddy play cricket in the garden with me and my brother and sisters. And ever Sunday I would be bowled after scoring a few, but not too many, runs. For some reason he used to win every time, but unlike me as a teenager he would never lose the ball in the neighbours' gardens.

Daddy had two styles of bowling. One was meticulous off-spin that, of course, never span when using a tennis ball on our rather rough and ready lawn, and just sat up nicely for a youthful slog into the flowerbeds. The other was a lethal quickie that looked just like the off-spin until the last moment – too late to do anything about – but which would often bowl the unsuspecting eight year old if on target.

At the age of about twelve, I remember being extremely proud to clean bowl Daddy, with my sister Mandy keeping wicket, with a Jeff Thompson style delivery I could never quite reproduce.

Daddy never got out on purpose unless the game was won, which a perfect way to play; no condescension, no easy way, just a challenge which when achieved was a great source of pride and honour.

On holiday with our friends the Grundys we had some marathon matches roping in mothers, siblings and even passing spectators and visiting great aunts, but the essential battle was the same: fathers against sons, and although there were five sons onto two fathers it was a great tussle.

I remember a game for Pontefract RAFA Club when I was thirteen, where although we lost dismally, the Enrights ended up as the two top scorers.

Duncan Enright

Many have heard of Derek's great love of dogs. He battled hard for Sammy, our Staffordshire Bull Terrier to be allowed into the House of Commons. He twice entered Sammy into the House of Commons Dog of the Year. Unfortunately, Sammy and he did not win – by the time of the judging, Sammy had already dragged his entrance sash through several flower beds and consequently was not looking his best. However with the family Dad maintained and outward ambivalence towards the many dogs which sat in his chair and shat on his carpets. "It's your mother's bloody dog," he would cry while battling with Sammy who had a fondness for biting his shoe laces.

The first dog I remember was Busby, who unfortunately turned out to be deaf. This was no real misfortune for Busby, more really for his owner. The curious habit that Enright dogs seem to have of running off was exacerbated in Busby's case by the fact that he would not come when called – or more accurately didn't hear you when you called. This led to many comical scenes at both Epsom and Pontefract race courses. Dad would have to sprint after Busby waving his arms in the hope of catching the dog's eye. The shouts he emitted served no purpose apart from to let passers by know that he was not mad. He developed as a result a reputation as an expert dog handler, so when a stray found its way into an electricity substation near Pete Hanson's home, it was Derek they called.

After Busby, we owned two boxer dogs, Polly and her daughter Jubilee. Polly was sly and proud – she would bite us children if we ever fell out of line but mostly paid due deference to my father. Jubilee, unsurprisingly born in 1977, was greedy. To the annoyance of us all she would eat anything left unattended. Easter eggs were not a tradition in our household. There was no ideological or religious reason behind this, just a practical one. Easter eggs did not survive. Jubilee ate them.

One fateful Christmas I inadvertently forgot to put the stilton back in the larder. Needless to say Jubilee ate it and left the remains scattered on the kitchen floor. When my father discovered the mess he flew into what only can be described as a violent rage. He found the cowering Jubilee, dragged her by the collar with her rear end trying to hold fast to the stone floor and proceeded to rub her nose into what remained of the stilton. Thereafter, she was not cured but was certainly more cautious in her thieving habits.

So when people talk of his great love of dogs, I say nothing. He certainly loved the long walks. The dogs were also the perfect cover for flatulence. My father never farted, although our dogs seemed uncontrollably smelly. And when Sammy was not trying to lick his face as he slept or running around in excitement at the merest hint of a prospective walk, he spoke almost fondly of him.

Perhaps it is fitting that the Staffordshire Bull terrier that survived his master keeps his own memory of Derek Enright. He has taken my father's old boots and uses them as a play thing in the garden.

Simon Enright

During the Winter of 1969 I was living at 9 Crest Mount, Carleton, Pontefract, and was safely tucked up at home with a roaring fire watching a football match. Outside it was pouring with rain and I could hear it beating on the windows but, above the noise, I heard the flap on the letter box close and saw a figure disappearing down the drive. It was Derek Enright and he was drenched. I quickly went into the hallway to find he had posted an election manifesto.

At that time Carleton had a ward of its own and Derek was canvassing and delivering for whoever was the candidate. I immediately rang his wife, Jane, to ask if I could have a word with Derek and she said he would ring me back that evening. When he rang me later I asked him for a form to join the Labour Party. He delivered a form by hand the next day, and I have been a member of the Party, and active in Local Government since 1973 to this day. What caused me to join was the sight of seeing someone working so hard while I was sat back relaxing. That was 26 years ago.

Tom Brennan

It is over twenty years ago, but I remember it as if it were yesterday. Quite how I became involved will always be a mystery, suffice it to say I knew Derek, so perhaps that's all it took! It was his first venture into politics in Pontefract, and he was hoping to be elected as a representative on the Pontefract Borough Council. So here we were, two first timers. I arrived and was handed a bundle of election pamphlets and pointed in the direction of a row of houses. "Easy" I thought, "simply post them through the letter box". I should have known it wasn't that simple. I was expected to knock on the door, introduce myself, and ask if we could count on their vote at the forthcoming election. I wasn't feeling too happy about this and Derek, seeing a lady in distress, said "Come with me Rosie, I'll show you how it's done". And so began the knocking on endless doors, and the opening and closing of gates. We always closed gates even if they had been left open. "Hello, I'm Derek Enright and I'm standing as your local councillor at the election. Can I count on your vote?" He was just so natural and sincere that he made it look incredibly easy. That early summer we were out most nights canvassing. We usually finished up at the Labour Club for a pint before we made our way home. It was a good campaign, such a pity we lost!

Rosie O'Kane

Joe Harper, MP for Pontefract and Castleford, had died in office from over work as a Whip in Callaghan's Labour-Lib Government, so the selection of a candidate to fight this safe seat was a high priority. There was a lot at stake. I was close to Derek as a family friend but I had fought alongside Geoff Lofthouse when the Labour Party had split at the seams in 1969 so I had a complicated decision to make. I had to throw what bit of weight I had at the back of one of them.

That night I argued strategically more than on principle. Derek tried to move that Pontefract put up two constituency candidates. I argued that we should only have one, because two from one district would split the Pontefract vote. I therefore moved the amendment that one candidate should go forward from both of the town's wards – it was a crucial decision as far as Derek was concerned. The members went for one candidate and in a fight out Derek lost 26 to Geoff's 86 votes.

Derek had cause to be resentful. He was a local man, an intellectual and he had a sound pedigree. His working class credentials were immaculate, and he had been a Party organiser.

As we walked away from the table after the ballot results had been announced, Derek caught up with me. "Do you want a drink?" "That would be nice", I said, "but I have to tell you this. I didn't vote for you".

"I never thought you would" he said with a laugh.

To me that generosity of spirit is unusual in anyone, but in a politician it has got to be unique.

Brian Lewis

When a distinguished Labour politician came to the area, Derek would give me a ring and ask me if I would like to go with him. I met lots of politicians such as Peter Shore and David Owen. Michael Foot was coming to Castleford Trades and Labour Club. "I'll pick you up at quarter past" said Derek.

Derek lived on his wits and never arrived early for anything, if he could get there on time. If I have a lift or an appointment I am waiting there half an hour early. Derek's car comes tearing round the corner at twenty five past. He arrives just in time to get the last parking space, and to walk out two paces ahead of Michael Foot.

Pat Brennan

I am currently President of the Pontefract RAFA club, and it is there that I met Derek. He did not serve in the RAF but was a 'friend' member of the club. Because of his services to the club he was made an Honorary Life Member several years ago. On the 50th anniversary of VE day he was resplendent in top hat and tails leading the entertainment. I certainly was unaware that he was unwell.

Harold Robinson

I remember a figure in top hat and tails brandishing a plastic bucket which he used to collect donations for charity from motorists entering Pontefract Park on RAFA Gala Days! He also compered party nights sometimes in Good Old Days style, and acting as auctioneer at our Harvest Festivals with his usual panache. There were also wonderful parties: seeing Derek and Jane off to Guinea Bissau, and the annual New Year's Eve events at his home which were attended by a wide range of people of all ages and backgrounds.

Another regular event was the family, along with any others they could enlist, doing the round of pubs, clubs and the like at Christmas singing carols to raise money for charity.

Derek's enthusiasm and confidence spanned everything he undertook, including playing cricket, as at the weekend spent in Oxford when Pontefract took on the Rest of the World to celebrate Duncan's impending wedding. His first ball to me was a steepling, ultra-slow off-break which, of course, I could not resist trying to hit out of the ground. I missed it and was lucky to survive to face yet more similar deliveries! The match finished in a tie and in the evening all participants dined at a Mexican restaurant. We finally landed at the student's bar at Wadham, well inebriated, and proceeded heartily to sing a wide range of songs, some of which, to say the least, were of dubious origin. The American tourists present thought it was a wonderful example of English culture!

John Gough

When a trio of teachers got together for a good pint and a game of cards in a relaxed atmosphere, it became clear that Colin with his keyboard, Pat with his guitar and Derek with his distinctive voice and wit, would at some stage become the people to lead the entertainment which at that time the RAFA club so sadly lacked.

Derek and Pat hit upon the idea of using a well-known tune as a vehicle for the words that they wrote to highlight yearly achievements as well as a golden opportunity to take witty sideways swipes at the Committee. When word got around that Enright, Brennan and Birch were performing, it was a case of standing room only. The seats went in the first minutes of the club opening.

There was always a wonderful buffet and a raffle and then what everyone had been waiting for. I can see them, even as I write. Colin, with his pint perched on his keyboard, Pat sitting on the edge of a table, guitar at the ready and Derek with a microphone clutched in his hand, his face full of innocent merriment, ready to announce the Order of Service. People stood shoulder to shoulder as they waited to see if they would be mentioned in dispatches! If you got a mention, you had arrived! If you didn't, there was always next time to look forward to.

> You may just have heard of
> McCartney and Lennon
> But they aren't half as good
> As our Enright and Brennan!

Lesley Atkinson

Derek has to be one of the most uninhibited people that was ever born. At Monk Fryston Hall he decided to lead the family in a bunch of children's action songs. There we were, all dressed up for dinner in an elegant restaurant, pretending to be elephants and other such animals. Derek was the only person who could play a two-handed action song and drink a pint of beer at the same time.

His niece, Jennifer, remembers him trying to sell her in Marks and Spencer. He held her up on his shoulders and said rather loudly: "Child for sale. Who wants to buy a child." Needless to say nobody did. She seems to think it was because she was priceless, but others have their doubts. The rest of the group tried to sneak out quietly.

As everyone knows, Derek enjoyed singing. Once while coming back from a London play he decided to test his vocal cords and co-ordination by tap dancing and singing "I Got Rhythm" on a park bench. He then proceeded to pick up a stick and ran along with it dragging it along a metal fence. On such occasions people tried to pretend they weren't with him.

The Boggett Family

"What was it" I hear you ask me, "set that man apart from the rest?"
"Was it his charisma, his commitment to life, his zest?"
Perhaps it was his caring and sharing disposition
That attracted so many people to his idealistic vision.

In County matters, European goals or Third World affairs,
That man brought personal qualities which really were quite rare.
Compassion, understanding and a clarity of mind
With a Christian attitude of kindness which you don't very often find.

Eventually to Parliament his political path progressed,
As MP for Hemsworth and Featherstone, his constituents were surely blessed,
Representing those Labour areas in that customary and resolute fashion
Winning the hearts of people as he debated with knowledge and passion.

"But what was it" I hear you ask me, "that set that man apart from the rest?"
Let's face it, having known that man, we would not need to have guessed,
It was surely the exemplary way that he simply lived his life
Sharing it so closely with Jane, his loyal wife.

And finally, to that man, Derek Enright, who deserves so great a tribute
Who was taken from us early yet had so much to contribute,
Well done, faithful servant, the Lord will say, and that is really why it
Seems apt to quote that Latin phrase: Fidem Servavit.

Colin Birch

When he came back from teaching in Surrey to teach at St Wilfrid's, he taught my children and so I know how good a teacher he was and how much he was appreciated by both staff and pupils. A couple of years ago I was honoured to be invited to play organ at church and I quizzed Derek about his favourite hymns. One we came up with was "Make me a Channel of your Peace". The words include:

Where there is hatred let me sow love,
Where there is injury, your pardon, Lord,
Where there's doubt, true faith in you,
Where there's despair in life, let me bring hope,
Where there is darkness, only light,
Where there is sadness, ever joy.
Grant I may never seek
So much to be consoled as to console,
To be understood, as to understand,
To be loved, as to love with all my soul.

Derek lived his life as near to that prayer of St Francis of Assisi as anyone I have known.

In recent years we spent two evenings a week playing cards at the RAFA club in Pontefract, where he was made an honorary life member, and I will miss the coppers I sometimes won from him. He was totally honest, and never did less than his best whatever he did and for whomsoever he did it.

Ray Valente

Leeds to Europe

Derek Enright – Our Man in Europe

Greetings from Strasbourg! In June it all sounded very romantic going to Luxembourg for the Socialist Group meeting, then Strasbourg for the first directly elected European Parliamentary Assembly. By the end of July I wondered why I had left security and the imminent prospect of an exciting headship, sharing each day with my family in a settled existence, for a nomadic life amid people who did not know how to conduct business in a proper fashion.

It was well illustrated late one evening by the interpreters. My translation headphones were switched on to them when one of our British politicians came in heatedly, after an Italian whose excited gestures did not match the cool translation on the earphones.

From our translation box, in addition to this MEP's impassioned speech, we heard from the interpreter, "Oh... he's going over the same...ground again! I'm fed up of this...job, I want something to eat and get home to sleep." The moment was further enlivened by another MEP asking: "Is the British translation I heard on the headphones correct?"

But September came, the committee work started and I remembered my aims and beliefs - a strong feeling for the Third World. Some 70% of the world population suffers from chronic under nourishment, and 24% from starvation. Put another way, it means, according to the World Bank report, that 17 million children under the age of five will die of hunger and in all, 58 million people will starve to death in 1979 alone.

The full Parliament had a seven-hour debate on how to tackle this problem. The United Nations agreed that each country should reach 0.7% of its national product in aid. The Community is a rich trading bloc, and yet only the tiny Netherlands with 0.85 (in 1977) has reached that figure.

Derek and Tom Megahy had gone out for a meal following some Brussels debate or other. The restaurant was good and as they sat down Derek turned to Tom and said: "Do you fancy a bottle of wine?" Well, Tom didn't know much about wine so he replied "You choose and we'll split the cost." Derek chose.

They were just getting down to drinking when one of the Italian Socialists passed and noticed the bottle. "I congratulate you Signor Enright; one of the best vintages in Italy."

"That's a bit surprising," said Derek," considering the cost."

"How much?" asked Tom.

"A lot less than £6". With that he got his calculator out and tapped in the figures once again.

"Well that doesn't seem a lot," Tom replied.

"Sorry Tom," said Derek, "I seem to have got the decimal point in the wrong place. It looks as if it's £56.45. Did you say we should split the cost?"

Derek was better at Greek and Latin than at sums.

Fred Pennington

That is the legend told in the Labour Clubs; this is the real story. When Derek and I were first elected in 1979 it took some time to adjust to dealing with Belgian or French currency all the time. This sometimes led to difficulties. As an indirect result of that, both Derek and I acquired a very high status, especially amongst our continental colleagues, as being wine connoisseurs of the first order. In fact, they were utterly amazed that two members from Yorkshire should be so absolutely knowledgeable about quality wines. Really it all happened by a combination of accident and ignorance. Derek and I went for lunch in a Brussels restaurant sharing a table with Ann Clwyd, now in the House of Commons, and Paulo Falcone, the Italian General Secretary of the Socialist Group. As we were eating fish, I asked Derek to order a bottle of white wine, which he promptly did. It was a nice wine, a bit sweet for my taste, but I remember saying to Derek "Jean (my wife) would like this, I might take a few bottles home".

Fortunately, I never got round to that. When we were drinking the wine, I noticed the look of admiration on the face of Paulo Falcone, who really was an expert on wine. He leaned forward and said, "I really must congratulate you on your choice of wine, you know that is the most original white wine you can drink with fish". We both felt very pleased and for the first time looked at the name of the wine. It was called Chateau d'Yquem, not that that meant anything to us quite frankly. When the bill came, we settled it in Belgian francs, which still seemed to have the characteristics of monopoly money at that time. Going back in the plane that evening, however, it began to dawn on us that it had been a very expensive lunch. Derek passed the bill to Barry Seal, another of our colleagues, who, having looked at it said the meal wasn't expensive, but our bottle of wine cost in the region of £60! Afterwards we found out it was one of the most exclusive and expensive of French wines.

As the story got around of course Derek and I were credited with tremendous knowledge of wine and for months afterwards we were confidentially asked our advice on which would be the appropriate wine to us. Of course being good politicians we confidently pronounced on many wines we didn't know anything about rather than have to tell the whole story of how we blundered into this one. It was always fun being with Derek and highly appropriate that we should both have ended up in this kind of situation.

Tom Megahy

The Golden Delicious, like Margaret Thatcher, was at once the pride of the greengrocer and a sign of the new freedom of the early 80s. It bruised rarely, polished up well, was sickly green with no fleck of red, had a sharp bite but no taste. Just like Margaret Thatcher. Also like the Iron Lady, it was flavour of the month in Strasbourg, as France was the home of this particular pomme.

The British competitor to the green menace was the good old Cox's Orange Pippin. The British apple tasted better, lasted longer, and had distinctive red markings. So it was adopted by the Labour Party in the person of Derek Enright, MEP. He resolved to take a bagful over to Strasbourg to show the rest of Europe that it wasn't only the Parti Socialiste that could raise an admiring "Core!" at the sight of a pippin.

Unfortunately at four in the morning, when leaving for his flight to Strasbourg, he couldn't find the apples under piles of washing and other family detritus. Instead of cancelling the press conference he had arranged, he made up a tale of four hungry children back in Yorkshire falling on the apples with delight, thus depriving him of a precious photo call for the Britapple. This new story delighted the papers, who proceeded to take photos of the four of us slavering over apple bowls, and provided the perfect boost for the good old Pippin.

Duncan Enright

It was a Friday, Sarah was very ill with cancer and I was standing at the window of the ward in Pontefract Infirmary, when I saw Derek approaching, obviously just back from Brussels or Strasbourg. I saw him bend down and pick some daffodils from the flower bed. In minutes he was up in the ward, presenting Sarah with the blooms.

I walked with him down the corridor to let him out. "They were lovely flowers," I said, "Where did you get them?"

He didn't pause, "Duty Free," he replied.

Geoff Lofthouse

During his time in the EP, he was one of the leading members in the fight for Brussels as our seat. I remember his motion that we should never have another plenary in Luxembourg – and his fairness and warmth and his sense of humour and kindness were always in evidence.

I last met him in the Commons last year. Although we are on opposite political sides, he showed more friendliness and interest than many of my Tory colleagues!

Anthony Simpson

I managed to nip in to visit Derek recently when I was on mission in London. I was shocked when I saw him, he looked so old, but he was still the same underneath and we had a great chat about our trip to Jamaica in 1983. I remember the German interpreter, who was head of the team and very bossy. She wanted me to tell Derek off for wearing sandals and t-shirts during our official visits. But I refused – Derek's speeches were always so brilliant and so appropriate that he always established a rapport with our interlocutors, it didn't matter what he wore!

Olive Dalmonte

Many people would have seen Derek's well-deserved and yet unexpected election to the House of Commons in 1991 as representing the pinnacle of his career. Yet I think that at least equally important to Derek was his participation, as the representative for Leeds, in the first-ever directly elected European Parliament in 1979.

It was in that year that I first met Derek, during the period immediately prior to the European elections when we had both been chosen as Labour candidates. Very poor results for Labour meant that, in the end, only a handful of us were elected but despite our numerical weakness, Derek quickly became one of the most prominent of the new MEPs. Indeed if European parliamentary activities had been reported and broadcast on anything like the scale of Westminster at that time Derek would have become a household name.

He was dynamic and active at every level in the Parliament and particularly in the Chamber where his distinctive and sonorous voice somehow managed to triumph over the stultifying effect of the simultaneous translation system.

In the European Parliament he assiduously pursued the concerns he held most dear – the interest of his Yorkshire constituents; his long standing commitment to the development of the Third World and his belief in our common European future. He also, as an early example of European "New Man", spoke on behalf of Labour MEPs on Women's rights issues – an area where the European Community and the European Parliament itself were to acquire a particularly good record of action.

Derek's sense of humour was always greatly in evidence in his interventions some of which spectacularly demolished his opponents – as the leading German Christian Democrat had reason long to remember when his hopes of becoming President of the European Parliament were scuppered for a number of years as a result.

Derek's period of office in the European Parliament coincided with a difficult time for Labour MEPs politically – particularly for the close knit group of us which held what was then the minority position on Europe within our Party – but Derek never once wavered in his conviction that a constructive approach to Europe was fully compatible with the Labour Party and with Democratic Socialism. That conviction was translated into many different constructive activities in the Parliament and Derek made many contacts across the national and political divides, forging particularly good friendships with outstanding MEPs – like

Jacques Delors who was subsequently to occupy such prominent roles both in the government of their own country and within the European Commission.

Socially Derek was always the life and soul of the European Party! To borrow Donald Dewar's memorable description of the late John Smith, Derek could start a party in an empty restaurant – and in Strasbourg frequently did. The commercial prospects of a modest eatery – "L'Orient" – dramatically improved the day Derek walked in, followed shortly afterwards of large numbers of MEPs, interpreters and staff. It was to become a great centre for politics and conviviality and even for fine singing – from John Hume, Ken Collins and others. Without Derek however it would have been nothing.

Joyce Quin

After deselection by the Old Guard in Leeds, Derek was invited to fight the then hopeless seat of Kent East in the 1984 European Elections. Typically he agreed. At the time the Miners' Strike was in full swing. Within the Euroconstituency were a handful of Kent coal mining villages, also caught up in the strike.

At a public meeting Derek addressed a group of miners which included a large number of Yorkshire, Scots and Geordie descent who had moved to the area. One great bone of contention in the press at the time was that Arthur Scargill, the miners' leader, was relying on a vote taken some time previously to provide a mandate to continue the strike, and much of the media plus a large section of the Labour Party was calling for a new ballot of all mineworkers to "validate" the industrial action.

At the public meeting Derek was not in the mood for anything but all-out attack. "They say we need a ballot" he said. "Let's give them a ballot; let's vote Labour in the European Elections!" Luckily they did; after a vigorous campaign Labour came a strong second behind the Tories. This was significant in a year when Labour lost ground throughout the South to the Social Democratic Party, and Kent East bucked the local and national trend. It also led to Labour victory in Kent East, just two elections later, which has been attributed by many locally to the strong fight put up in earlier years which placed Labour within striking distance of success.

Duncan Enright

My warmest memory of Derek Enright goes back about ten years when we were both members of the European Parliament. Like me he was involved in the problems of the Third World and attended gatherings of the developing countries to which the European Community gives aid under the Lome Convention. But here the similarity ended. His generous and tolerant spirit made him popular in all parts of the Parliament while my abrasive temperament made me many political enemies.

In 1981, the Lome countries met in Sierra Leone, on of the poorest countries in Africa. I had outraged my European colleagues by protesting at the lavishness of the allowances we European delegates received and by spontaneous agreement they decided to cold shoulder me. On my first day I breakfasted alone at the hotel and went down to the beach for a solitary swim, reconciled to being sent to Coventry for the entire week. But as I took my lonely walk along the sandy palm studded beach two warm welcoming voices greeted me from the beach's shady fringe: "Hello Barbara. Here we are. Come and join us." It was Derek and Jane Enright genuinely delighted to have my company.

It was beginning of a happy week in which we went everywhere together and led to a deeply affectionate friendship. I realised then that Derek and Jane might be gentle people, but they had guts. They did not give a damn what other people thought of me.

Later when Derek became the European Commission's representative in another desperately poor African country, Guinea Bissau, he did not change. Jane, as always, identified herself with his uphill task. When my niece and I visited him in his lonely outpost we could see the size of it. On the Sunday of our stay Derek said he was going to attend mass in the nearby Catholic leper colony. Of course, Protestants though we were, we insisted on accompanying him. What do sectarian differences matter in the face of human suffering?

I use to tease Derek about his tolerance but I can see today how Northern Ireland could do with a large chunk of it and that tolerance sometimes demands more courage than intolerance.

So I salute a man of principle and his equally courageous wife. Together they were always prepared to risk a great deal to build a better world.

Barbara Castle

Brussels to Bissau

On 28 October 1987, Derek became the first foreigner ever to be awarded the Order of Merit in Guinea Bissau.

It was with deep sadness that we learned of the premature death of Mr Derek Anthony Enright, former representative of the European Commission in Guinea Bissau. Possessing great human and professional qualities, Derek Enright, when he was in my country, exemplified an elevated vision of the appropriate role for a United Europe in its relations with Developing Countries, especially those on the continent of Africa.

The people and government of Guinea Bissau, and I myself, remember Derek Enright as an intelligent, determined worker who did all in his power to accomplish the mission of co-operation and friendship which brought him to my country. We have lost a sincere friend who left us such pleasant memories and I send our deepest sympathy to the European Commission and in particular, to his wife Jane, and his children. We assure them of our friendship and best wishes.

His Excellency Senhor Joao Bernardo Vieira,
President of the Republic of Guinea Bissau

The journey from Pontefract to Bissau was not one made by many people, and therefore the transport links were poor. Even to phone Bissau was less than straightforward, and meant a call to the international operator, who then called the Portuguese operator, who made a radio call and patched you through to the one and only Guinea Bissau operator. This individual, a young man in search of an overseas scholarship, knew all callers on a first name basis. He switched the caller through to the European Delegate's residence. Too often the line broke leaving both sides with big bills for a short burst of conversation.

The only reliable UK link with Bissau was the radio, and the BBC World Service was a lifeline for my parents. They listened to every show, without discrimination. For the first time in years we children could talk on an equal footing about the Top 40 pop charts with our parents as the Chart Show, like all others, provided a clear but rare taste of Britain and was therefore essential listening.

Transport, like electricity (supplemented by a local generator which had to be fired up each evening as the City supply failed), was erratic. Air Portugal TAP ran a weekly service to Bissau airport which, though towered over by a state-of-the-art radar system courtesy of the East German government, had the crudest of baggage handling services and a huge warehouse without walls for a terminal building. Flights were frequently delayed, causing frustration for the many people who came to meet every plane, whether or not they knew anyone aboard.

On one occasion Daddy endured the incredible journey home, connection delayed as ever at Lisbon airport and taking over a day to get from darkest African sub-Sahara to brightest super-Humber Yorkshire. As luck would have it he got into Pontefract at about 10pm, and so just in time to get to the Pontefract RAF Association Vulcan Club for last orders, which he enjoyed all the more for the first pint of Webster's Pennine Bitter for 6 months and the company of so many good friends.

Duncan Enright

I write of 1986. Derek had just arrived in Guinea Bissau as Ambassador for the EEC and we had already met at a few occasions. Derek wanted to know where he could go for a swim in the sea, where he could find a beach? The Guinea Bissau coast exists mainly of mangrove swamps and due to the 5 metre difference between high and low tide, one hardly finds beaches. Instead the borders of the estuary are muddy slopes of sometimes a few metres wide, which provoked Derek saying "Water, water everywhere but no place to swim."

The answer came from a German sociologist who had some historical books of then Portuguese Guinea. It showed pictures of the beach at Prabis with nice little straw huts for shade. Prabis is only 25 km from Bissau so Derek suggested we should go there. If there was a beach in 1935 there must be something there now.

Help came from a Mr Franzetti, a Senegalese building contractor of Italian origin who had a plane which he used to fly back his family to Dakar each weekend. Ten minutes after take off from Bissau airport we were already there and from the air we saw a white beach and a lighthouse. We flew over the mangrove swamp and clearly recognized the road that others were not able to find. It was completely overgrown by mangroves. Derek and I were determined we would rediscover the Prabis beach.

That Sunday, we left in a party of 12, in two four-wheel drives, equipped with machetes, but also with an ice box full of cold beer, food, sun lotion and swimming trunks. We drove until the road nearly ended. We continued on foot but progress through the mangroves was slow.

Soon we had blisters on our hands from the machetes and after a few hundred metres, Derek, dripping with sweat, called me over and said that at this rate we would never get there. Inspiration struck. He looked at the creek beside the road and suggested that we get in the water and let the current take us to the beach. We tied our shoes around our necks and jumped in carefully holding the ice box with the cold beer.

About a hundred metres down stream we heard shouting. Our first thought was of crocodiles or snakes but then it became clear: there was somebody who could not swim! Still floating in the water we decided to climb out of the creek on the other side where the mangroves appeared to be less dense. Knee deep, we went into the mud, and when we made it to the mangrove bank we were covered in mud from our feet to our chests.

We called the others for a short meeting. Some wanted to give up but Derek was determined: we had seen this beach from the air, it could not be far away. The mangrove on this bank was only a few metres wide and after cutting a path we found a mud plane stretching a few hundred metres. This was it. We started to walk towards what we thought was the promised beach. The few hundred metres took us about an hour: the mud plane that appeared solid was as soft as a sponge. It sucked our legs up to our knees and it was extremely hard work to move forward. The thought of a swim in the ocean kept us going but we tried not to think of how we could get back before dark.

Still with no beach in sight and rather exhausted we sat down for another meeting. Derek insisted that we try for at least another 15 minutes. We also decided to take some more weight from the ice box! Being one of the tallest, two minutes later I spotted the lighthouse. Five minutes later we heard the waves. Another five minutes later we were floating in the blue ocean, fully dressed, washing kilos of mud out of our clothes. It was the most rewarding swim I have ever had.

As we started for home, a little boy appeared. We asked him how he got there and where he lived. He answered that his village was very near to where we left the cars and that there is a path. Could he kindly show us the way? Of course he could.

Fifteen minutes later after a very easy walk (no mud at all, we had to put our shoes on again) we were back in our air-conditioned Nissan Patrols. 45 minutes later, back in Bissau, we dropped Derek at his house, wishing him a good night's sleep. "Oh no, no time for sleep," he said, "At 1700 hours, there is an important meeting of the Association of Non-Governmental Organisations. I've been invited and if I take a quick shower, I can just make it in time." What energy this man had. Mind you, it was Sunday!

Jan Van Maanen

It started as a joke and ended as a holiday of a lifetime. Like many other people, when Derek said his next appointment was in Guinea Bissau, we said, "Where?"; rushed to the World Atlas, then said, "We'll have to drop in to see you."

On Derek and Jane's first home leave we were reminded of our promise and typically told how welcome we would be. Indeed we were, even to the extent of their travelling more than 250 miles over very poor roads to meet us in Ziguinchor in South Senegal, so cutting the cost of our travelling and enabling us to see more of the Bissau country. So many pictures and snippets of knowledge still spring to mind from that holiday.

We visited evangelical missions supported by the EEC and the Tear Fund. What a variety! There was an urban one, which included a car mechanics' apprenticeship scheme involving a man from Morley. There was a general medical mission with mother and baby clinic, run by a woman doctor and a woman nurse. Between them they had been in Bissau over 40 years. There were men repairing the holes in the roads, using termite mounds. This was often part of their community service; a good alternative to prison.

We were invited into a traditional African (Palhotas) hut, the home of the EEC Delegation cook, Bequinte, to see their new baby. She was named Mandy after one of Derek's daughters. We met many of the visitors who called to discuss with Derek the problems of the country and in what form aid should be given. I was tremendously impressed with Derek's fluency in languages. We visited the wood carving school near to Derek and Jane's house where young orphans were being taught a money-spinning skill. That was where we bought many of our souvenirs.

Then one Saturday evening we went to the old Portuguese style cathedral. When we came out Derek commented that it was the very first time he'd seen his car under a lit up street light. That week the government had made a determined effort to get electricity working in the centre of the capital and so celebrate an international conference being held there.

Wherever we travelled, by car or walking, Derek would tell us so much about what we saw. That was because he had immersed himself into the history and needs of the country in order to do his job. Derek also took great pleasure in showing what could be done with international co-operation and aid: a refurbished ferry at Farim; a new school at Mansoa; a mental hospital in Bissau, and a bridge at Bambadinca. He was precise and scholarly but he could also make us laugh at the idea of one country donating snow ploughs to keep the airport runway clear in winter in a country just 12 degrees above the equator. We relaxed – we laughed and had fun – yet we also learnt a lot without realising it. That was Derek's way.

Brenda Macaskill

In the summer of 1987 I spent a few days in Bissau accompanying my mother and father, the British Ambassador for that region of West Africa. We stayed with Derek in the EC Delegate's residence. Knowing Simon from Atlantic College I was keen to meet his father, and immediately recognised the mischievous twinkle in his eye. My parents, however, had already experienced the benefit of his diplomatic skills on their first visit to Bissau.

Driving innocently around the unmarked streets one evening, they unwittingly passed through a car-free residential area. Outraged, the civic-minded Bissauans attempted a citizens' arrest. Of course, the culprits, my parents, did not understand and, thinking they were being attacked by car-jackers, fled. Unfortunately, they only managed to make the situation worse, not least by racing at full speed over a memorial to Amalcar Cabral, hero and martyr of Guinea Bissau's independence.

It is not often that Britain turns to Europe for assistance but, when the British Ambassador turned up on his European counterpart's doorstep, pursued by an angry mob, help was at hand. Explaining that their prey were newcomers, who didn't know what they were doing, Derek pacified the mob in a moment, and soon, incredibly, they were all smiles and handshakes. My parents took a little longer to calm down but needless to say, he managed that too.

Rory Macrae

Derek Enright – The European Cup

The damp, dank fog of a winter's day in Yorkshire brings happy memories of hot, humid days in Guinea Bissau, as I shiver, wrapped in my woollies. But then, the hot, humid days of a November in Bissau used to bring happy memories of damp, dank days in Yorkshire as I sweated in my shirt sleeves. Here central heating or a good coal fire brings bliss, there it was air conditioning or a delicious breeze from the sea. What different worlds they are – and the economic climate is as different as the physical.

There the battle is to get enough to find the rice to feed the family; here in the shops and supermarkets there is a bewildering array of goods being calmly pursued by crowds of people. Here there is a great expression of dismay over the gaps in the National Health Service; there the import of a simple 50p medicine which could save a life cannot be afforded.

But for me the biggest difference is being able to speak English all day – and almost relearn the language. And all those white faces! How to distinguish one from the other?

What things stand out in my mind? There was the hospital run by Franciscans where I could go to Mass out of town between the Palestine Liberation Organisation's vegetable farm and a factory *built on a foreign loan with sufficient capacity to manufacture cars for export, but without the raw materials, let alone the electricity to go into production. A reminder that Palestinians are not just fighters, but farmers, and that loans kindly meant can bring debts without benefits. To the hospital itself the EEC gives food aid which means that their precious and scarce foreign currency can be spent on basic medicines. Mass there was warm and, stranger that I was, welcoming, even though the sign of peace was given by shaking hands with men and women without hands.*

An underdeveloped country? Yes, in some ways. But the chief driver of my delegation could speak four languages including French and Portuguese of the European languages and could add a good smattering of English with perfect pronunciation. Honesty? I find it difficult to remember that I could park my car and leave the keys in the ignition, let alone the door unlocked. Tolerance? The largest religion is Animist, followed closely by the Muslims and finally a minimal number of Christians, overwhelmingly Catholics. Nobody goes out to convert and all learn from each other. It is a single party state, but the range of views would cover the whole spectrum of our parties. And all the arguments are conducted with great charity.

Last year was the 30th anniversary of the signing of the Treaty of Rome and in agreement with all the other institutions of the EEC, the Commission arranged celebrations of the occasion not only in Europe but in those countries where the EEC is represented. We were given a restricted budget to salute the anniversary and a limited time to prepare. The temptation was to give a cocktail party for the leading members of the Government and the Diplomatic Corps and have a small exhibition with tape recordings of the speeches of Adenauer, Churchill, Schuman and the great European statesmen – exciting for the cognoscenti but not likely to be a crowd puller even in Europe!

Instead I decided that we (and that means on behalf of you, the citizens of Europe) should have a football cup to be played for by the top clubs of Bissau (there are just four of them!) But how to buy cup and medals in time? One plane a week flies to Lisbon, the nearest place to buy such honours. A friend was found to be flying out one week, another flying back the following week, and my order was duly despatched and delivered. The cup, as specified, was a splendid affair, almost 5ft tall,

gleaming, silvery and magnificently inscribed as "Taca Schuman"
celebrating co-operation between the EEC and Guinea Bissau. Some
might call it vulgar. Not I! It stood on display in a shop and gathered
great crowds.

The two semi-finals were full houses – or so I thought. The final, in the
main stadium, was something else again. We arranged for the twelve
flags of the Member States plus the flag of Guinea Bissau and the 12
starred flag of Europe to be hung round the ground. There was a carnival
atmosphere and the national radio carried reports on the match
throughout the day as the flags flew proudly in the centre of the city.

By the time it came to the big final, the ground was packed to
overflowing. The trees in the neighbourhood looked perilously close to
cracking under the weight of the spectators perched on them. Half the
Government, and the entire Embassies were ready in their seats.

It was a very entertaining game. Everybody was very partisan and the
underdogs won. The radio carried the whole match (there is no television
in Bissau) and I am willing to wager that as a result of that a greater
percentage of people in Guinea Bissau knew that it was the EEC's
birthday - and enjoyed the party! I felt like royalty presenting the cup. A
way had to be cleared through the celebrating supporters who swamped
the pitch. It was done by the police – all three of them! Eat your heart
out, Leeds United.

I shall not forget the pleasure that a European celebration gave to the
Guineans because of their endeavour and pride. I thank them.

Yorkshire Evening Post, 26 February 1988

Hemsworth to Westminster

Derek Enright – Maiden Speech

I pay tribute to my predecessor George Buckley. No one could but admire the fortitude with which he bore his last painful illness and the way in which at the same time he stuck to his constituency work which he performed with great conscientiousness. He had been equally conscientious as a councillor when I worked with him and he was a fine and scrupulous justice of the peace. I recall, and perhaps you recall too, Mr Deputy Speaker, that during one election period George Buckley was accused of being an extremist. He was extremely hurt by that and announced that he was a moderate and a patriot. I declare here and now that I intend to follow that same path. Above all, I should say that George was a family man. He looked after his family; he cared for them. I am sure that the House will join me in sending our condolences to his widow and children.

Because Hemsworth has always had a large Labour majority, it sounds like a great monolith, but it is very far from that. It is a series of villages in the south-east of Wakefield metropolitan district which were essentially rural in character. But over the years, because of coal mining and their transformation into pit villages, they have become rural areas with urban problems, with poor communications. But each village has a fierce patriotism. The patriotism is not to Hemsworth unless one lives in Hemsworth. To someone who lives in Upton, Upton is the centre of the universe. Perhaps Upton people are right to say that because they have a tremendous history. I am sure that they will have a tremendous future. They populate the world. It is said that one cannot go anywhere – I know that this was true in West Africa – without meeting someone from Upton who will give good and wise advice.

There is also the village of Ackworth, where Geoff Boycott took his first faltering steps at the crease to become the greatest cricketer that the world has ever seen and a great Yorkshireman. Ultimately, because we pray for him every night, he will change his politics.

The constituency has been destroyed because of the destruction of its industry, mining; a destruction that was completely unnecessary. We are left with real problems of unemployment and all that goes with that with the drifting away of hospital care so that everything is centred outside the constituency; with the drifting away of real jobs so that people have to move outside. One reason for that drifting away is that, as a result of the Government's failure to obey European Community rules, we are not getting the money that we should under RECHAR. Cato used to end all his speeches with the words, "Delenda est Carthago". I will conclude all my speeches with a plea for money from RECHAR. We have already sown the seeds of what needs to be done to bring about job regeneration in my area. The small extra amount of money for that purpose already approved by the Commission would make a tremendous difference.

The mining part of the community that I represent is extremely important, even though only one working pit is left. Our history and our traditions are in mining, and those traditions remain even when people move into other kinds of industry.

I want to consider for a moment the true price of coal. A very good friend of mine, George Gough, died last Saturday from emphysema. I pay tribute to the work done by my hon. Friend the Member for Pontefract and Castleford (Mr Lofthouse) in the area and promise that I will assist him in his fight. The true price of coal centres on the lack of safety that is to be found in the mines, which reflects the lack of concern that is often shown.

The fear the Frickley colliers have now is that when their mine is privatised – and they are convinced that will happen soon, unless there is a change of Government – safety standards will fall. They look forward to other assistance from Europe in respect of the social charter. The Minister said that the Government are waiting for certain European directives, but failed to mention that the Government are blocking several directives that would assist workers in my constituency. I think particularly of consultation on change, which must take place under the social charter but which has not been observed. The miners of Frickley have in no way been consulted over their futures. I warn again that I will be fighting for that, too.

Featherstone is another area that once relied on coal and it is also where I taught for 12 years as deputy head of a comprehensive school which I established. I am extremely proud of the comprehensive education system. My school vied with eight grammar schools and produced results better than any of them – and for many more children. That is why I am proud of the comprehensive system and why I will support my hon. Friend the Member for Leeds, Central (Mr Fatchett) in all his splendid work to make education once more a human thing with human values.

Also in Featherstone we have a rugby team which will win the cup this year. I look forward to the Prime Minister being present that day – but, of course, by then it will be a Labour Prime Minister. I will co-operate with and fight alongside my hon. Friend the Member for Rother Valley (Mr Barron) for the interests of coal and do all that I can to assist my party's energy team in that fight. I want to make sure that Hemsworth can continue to be proud of its history. I will rail against its present problems and I will certainly fight for its future.

Ended approx 6.39 pm

I didn't know Derek until he arrived here in the House and sat just in front of me. We strongly disagreed on the EU but that never stopped us being good friends. Derek, as you must know, simply did not make enemies and that was all part of his personality and probably his approach to life. When I heard that Derek was at St Thomas's I just strongly hoped that he would pull through, but life is unfair – probably Derek would not have agreed too much with that! – and he should have had at least another twenty years of life. He was a good man.

David Winnick

I first met Derek Enright when I was in the Young Socialists with Duncan. Sometimes we would meet at their house on Carleton Rd but I think at that stage Derek was an MEP and was away in Europe a lot of the time. After that I occasionally used to come across him at Labour Party events and he was always very friendly and showed a keen interest in what I was doing. Very shortly after he was appointed to stand for MP in Hemsworth I was rather surprised to receive a telephone call from him asking for my help. He had taken the unusual step of appointing a woman to be his election agent and thought as agent for Geoff Lofthouse I could give her a few tips on how to handle the traditional Labour Party male! Attitudes towards women have changed a lot in the last few years and women are actively encouraged to take on positions but at that time Derek was taking a brave step. Since then Jane Perry and I have become great friends and I feel I have Derek to thank for that friendship.

Kathryn Stainburn

I recall many years ago when Joe Harper was MP for Pontefract and Castleford, Derek was a delegate to the constituency meetings and always made valuable and responsible contributions in debates on policy making. Even in those far off days, he was destined to make his mark in politics. In 1973 he was elected to the West Yorkshire County Council, and made a significant contribution during his time there. He was subsequently elected as a Member of the European Parliament for Leeds, and served with distinction for five years.

He was then elected as the Member of Parliament for Hemsworth, after much controversy. He overcame these difficulties to serve the whole of the constituency as a popular and effective MP. His early death was a tragedy for the constituency and I am confident that Derek would have made his mark, had he lived to become a member of a future Labour Government.

Jack Smart

I have some happy memories of Derek both as a mischievous public speaker and also as someone to have on your side when the going got tough. I had been invited along with Derek to a dinner of the Catenian Society. As can happen I had got the feel of this rather formal event wrong: I turned up in a lounge suit when everybody was formally dressed for dinner. Derek was the speaker. Addressing the august gathering, he began: "There are only one or two people in this room tonight qualified to speak here on an occasion like this, and Colin Croxall, leader of Wakefield MDC isn't one of them; well just look at how he's dressed!" Of course these opening remarks caused a great deal of amusement but after this gentle leg pulling he went on to praise my work.

Another occasion was in more robust circumstances. I was called along to a public meeting at the Pretoria Working Men's Club, South Elmsall along with Derek, Tom Megahy MEP, and Jane Perry who was standing for the first time as a District Councillor. As leader of the District Council, I was the one perceived as responsible for all the wrongs of the District from the year dot and was the focus of all the hostility and aggression. At the end of the meeting a crowd of heavies came up to Derek and were threatening him and were saying if he expected their votes at the next General Election he should put pressure on me to do what they wanted. Derek didn't hesitate and immediately answered: "Right is right, no matter how many oppose it. Wrong is wrong, no matter how many speak up for it; and Councillor Croxall is right." He was a very honest and direct politician. He knew what was right and didn't mind saying so.

Colin Croxall

At the end of 1994 I had been waiting for a heart by-pass operation for some 14 months. One day on the news Mrs. Bottomley, the Health Minister, stated that no-one should wait longer than one year for such an operation. I decided to write to Derek to tell him of my case, and maybe give him some ammunition to get at the Tories. In a little more than a week Derek had replied to my letter to say that he had been in touch with my surgeon's secretary and that I should be in hospital in the next few weeks.

As I read the letter that morning and began to feel a little queasy at the thought of the operation, the telephone rang and the secretary told me that if I could come into the hospital that day the surgeon would do the operation. With no time to feel afraid I packed my bags and by early afternoon I was in the ward being shaved and starved for the next days ordeal.

The quadruple by-pass operation was, I am pleased to say, a complete success, and after some eight days I was back home being pampered by my wife and daughter.

About a month later as I was beginning to feel my feet again I saw in the local paper that Derek was holding one of his regular surgeries in the near-by library. I thought that I should appear in person and thank him for his undoubted help. After a short wait, I was ushered in to see Derek and his wife.

He didn't really know me personally so we shook hands and I said, "Mr Lumb."

"Sit down Mr Lumb," he replied. "What can I do for you?"

"Sorry to take up your time," I apologised, "but I've just come to thank you for the by-pass."

"Oh! Don't thank me yet Mr Lumb, we are still having objections from Ackworth. The road may be another 10 years yet."

"No, no," I laughed. "I mean my heart by-pass operation. It was a complete success."

It took a few moments for it to sink in. Then he looked up, saw me grinning and his face was a picture. He was also grinning broadly. "Ah!" he chuckled. "That Mr Lumb."

Tony Lumb

It is generally thought that the best cricket umpires are not noticed. They go about their business in an unobtrusive way, efficiently giving decisions when called upon and generally keeping control of the game. There are naturally exceptions to any general rule. One thinks of Dickie Bird. In the same category would come Derek Enright.

I have fond memories of Derek as an umpire. In his short time as a member of Parliament he became a regular umpire for the Lords and Commons cricket team. Naturally Derek was always scrupulously fair. But it is difficult to suggest that he was ever unobtrusive in the more traditional school of umpiring. With his straw hat and, with that mischievous look in his eye, Derek was always part of the game. He was always offering advice and opinions. He was as a cricket umpire exactly the same as in so many other activities: committed, fun-loving and part of the action, was the way in which Derek would describe his role as an umpire and in life more generally.

The Lords and Commons Cricket team will be less rich without Derek's presence. We will miss that hat, the laugh, the voice: all of the things which were simply Derek.

Derek Fatchett

In November 1987, a Conservative Secretary of State for Education took it upon himself to introduce an Education 'Reform' Bill that he said would revolutionise standards in state schools. The Rt Hon Kenneth Baker MP spotted his chance to enter the history books with a return to "Basics" and a re-introduction of traditional teaching methods. His Bill when first published gave the Government 250 new powers of central control over schools and colleges – I know because it was my job to count them on the morning of publication. The Bill was to introduce National Curriculum and testing as well as opt-out schools and city technology colleges. It soon began a tortuous passage through the House of Commons. For weeks the Government were harried by the opposition parties, with the rest of the education world in close support. The Government were told that the testing regime that they envisaged would not work – in 1993 it was completely overhauled. They were warned that opting out would be divisive and unpopular – only 1000 schools have become grant-maintained almost 8 years later.

But most of all the Government wanted to put the Labour Party on the spot over school standards. At every turn they tried to paint Labour MPs as being ignorant and preaching a drab uniformity of Comprehensive Schools. It was during one such long debate, in a standing Committee on the Education Reform Bill, that Derek so completely silenced the Tory critics. It is a memory that will stay fresh in the mind – the baying Conservative MPs with their slick suits and upper-crust accents, momentarily lost for words at the hands of a Northern Labour MP who could simply answer them back in Latin. It was the talk of the tea room for weeks.

Richard Margrave

Sir Nicholas Fairburn was in what we in the House call a "tired and emotional state". It was a quiet time of the evening and few people were in the debating Chamber when this well known Conservative eccentric having heard Derek use Latin shouted across, "I bet you can't sing in Latin". This was too much of a challenge. Without hesitation Derek broke into a rendition of the famous Beatles' classic, "Yellow Submarine". Whether he was translating on the spot or recalling an earlier translation, I do not know. Derek was fluent in the language, so either was possible. It was very impressive, but the dignity of the House of Commons is a precious thing and although I let him have a brief moment of glory, I could not let him get away with too much. As Speaker, I intervened:

"The Honourable Member has been here long enough to know that he is required to speak in English in this Chamber and also that singing is not part of the tradition of this place. I require him, therefore, to sit down and be silent."

He did sit, though afterwards he sought me out and in a very direct way said, "With friends like you, who needs enemies?"

Geoff Lofthouse

The translation into Latin of Yellow Submarine, which was reproduced in the House of Commons, does not represent a word-for-word rendering, but instead offers a version as might have been composed by one of the Classic poets. In the same way Eleanor Rigby, as offered on the CD "Exotic Beatles" (to which Derek contributed two tracks soon after the events in the House of Commons), takes as its theme the desperation of Anchises and Dido at the flight of Aeneas, ending "Omnes hic deserti, unde venerunt huc".

Duncan Enright

It is difficult to know just how far the news that Derek was the man who translated the Yellow Submarine into Latin travelled. There was a note in the Sunday Telegraph which said that when asked the name of her favourite Beatles number, Virginia Bottomley, who by her age has to be a first-generation fan, replied,

"A Yellow Submarine – but in Latin, sung by Derek Enright MP."
He had friends in all parties.

Terry Tuningley

Derek Enright – Yellow Submarine

In natali oppido
Erat homo nauticus
Qui inquit: "Habito sub aequoribus vitreis"
(Una) Habitamus sub vitreo, sub vitreo, sub vitreo
(Bis)   Habitamus sub vitreo, sub vitreo, sub vitreo

Navigamus usque ad sol
Quo erat mare vitreum
Habitamus in aquis sub navibus roseis
(Una) Habitamus sub vitreo, sub vitreo, sub vitreo
(Bis)   Habitamus sub vitreo, sub vitreo, sub vitreo

Amici nostri tuti illic
Etiam plures proximi
Incipimus canere una voce cuncti
(Una) Habitamus sub vitreo, sub vitreo, sub vitreo
(Bis)   Habitamus sub vitreo, sub vitreo, sub vitreo

I saw Derek only a few months ago in Brussels, when he was in the European Parliament with a Westminster delegation. I had slipped out of my office for a couple of minutes and when I came back he was sitting in my chair, claiming that there couldn't have been that many Kenninghams in the EP! He gave me a big hug and I thought what a kind, warm person he was. I promised to buy him lunch (or at least a coffee) the next time he came.

Derek obviously cared a great deal for other people. I'm sure his constituents would bear witness to that. I owe him a great deal for the example he has set as a representative to all people and for the encouragement he has given me personally within the Labour Movement.

Rachael Kenningham

Derek was one of those rare politicians with whom it was always a pleasure to do business, here at Yorkshire TV. He always turned up on time, always had something interesting to say, and cheerfully put up with our "sound bite" demands that he pack a complex argument into two minutes. We could always count on at least one bright spot in a programme if Derek was taking part - (even if he was talking English as opposed to singing Beatles in Latin!) He was a good friend to us here and our programmes will be the poorer without him. On a personal level we will miss his wit and wisdom as well as a kindly and astute source of political gossip and enlightenment.

Geoff Druett, Richard Whiteley & Charlotte Milligan

Derek was a fine man, a good man, genuinely liked and respected by all who knew him. At the Parliamentary Labour Party, when Doug Hoyle read out a tribute, people were moved and demonstrative in their affection for him.

Tony Blair

Epilogue

Many of us in Yorkshire will be saddened by news of Derek Enright's death on the eve of All Saints. He died in St. Thomas's Hospital in London, just opposite the House of Commons which has been his home as MP for Hemsworth for the last few years. He was a fine constituency MP much appreciated by the people of his home town. Before that he served as MEP for Leeds and as a European Community special advisor on the Third World. His first career was teaching (Classics) and he will be remembered with special affection by former pupils and colleagues of St. Wilfrid's Catholic High School, Featherstone, where in its early days he taught and he was Deputy Head.

To all he did, he brought an infectious enthusiasm and complete dedication. He loved his work, he loved his Catholic faith. His faith and his work were never separated. You knew that on any matter of principle he spoke from the clear background of his belief in God and his loyal and happy membership of the Church. People might not always agree with him, but they would always trust and respect him. There is something apt and consoling in his dying just before the feast of All Saints, which is the celebration of all those good people who go to meet God. May he rest in peace.

David Konstant, Bishop of Leeds

Sadly he came to the House of Commons too late in life to appear on the front bench, which he would have graced with wit and humanity. He understood the passion and the pain of his constituents, the people from whom he sprang. He articulated their fears after the pit closures and their hopes for a better tomorrow, elegantly, and never with malice.

He leaves behind a host of friends, all of whom have different but happy memories of how he touched their lives, recalling his puckish sense of humour, his self-deprecating smile which became half chuckle and half laugh, but above all his constant devotion to the principles of democratic socialism, and the Catholic faith in which he was born and died.

As he lay before the high altar, on his coffin were a crucifix , a copy of the gospels, and more particularly and significantly, his own well-thumbed missal.

Kevin McNamara

I met Derek on his first day of teaching at the John Fisher School when I was entering the Sixth Form. He was the first person to awaken my political, social and Christian conscience. The first task of the day was always to translate the leader of the Guardian into Latin and Greek. It was a great exercise for discerning the real meaning of the words of politicians and others.

Derek was a man who operated in three arenas. The first was intensely personal. He was a man of faith and love – with gifts of prophecy, language and knowledge which, though imperfect, yet gave a glimpse of greater things beyond sight. The second was the world stage. On the day of his funeral, we listened to the prayer for peace in Jerusalem, we remembered the funeral also taking place of another peacemaker Yitzhak Rabin. We rejoiced for them both and heard the words "Let us go to God's house".

The third arena is cosmic. What can bring us happiness? Many say: lift up the light of your face upon us, O Lord. Derek was not arrogant or cynical as the world can be in answering this question; he worked and strived for the values of the gospel and the kingdom to be more present in our world.

He was a teacher – by his gentle challenge; a pilgrim – who opened the way for others; and a reconciler – by his passion for and conviction about the truth.

May he rest in peace.

Peter Humfrey

Sarah was much on my mind during those last days of Derek's life. I had seen her decline and pass away and I had witnessed other deaths but none have I seen whose bravery during this critical period matched Derek's. He had come back from the Labour Party Conference and I had gone as a regular visitor across the Thames to his bedside in St Thomas' Hospital. He was frequently in my mind especially at night when I was in one of Parliament's dining rooms. As I glimpsed out, I could see the light of his NHS room – it was the top but one floor, third from the right.

Unlike many who die, Derek made it easy for the visitor. He mentioned death before you did, but continued to go on showing interest in what was happening in the world outside. He talked of the Shadow Cabinet elections (I had voted in proxy on his instructions), the PLP and a whole range of detailed parliamentary interests we shared. Death almost seemed irrelevant; although dying he was talking in the matter of fact way that I associate with him. I don't have to invent this quotation for it is word for word accurate, "Geoff" he said, "I'm going to die before the election. A pity really. I'd have liked to have been there".

The roof of Westminster Cathedral seemed to go up for ever and I have to admit to being nervous. The setting was awe-inspiring, three priests to either side of me, a young man to lead me in quiet dignity to the microphone and the congregation members of both political parties, media people and a real mixed bag of Pontefract folk. There were his fellow Catholics, Anglicans, like myself, non-conformists and here and there an agnostic or even atheist or two. One thing brought them together: their love and affection for a remarkable man.

Although I would speak as I found him; honourable, sincere, amusing, brave – a friend. I was not sure if I could carry this one off. I knew how easily my emotions could take over. My personal uncertainty however was held in check by what I saw in front of me. Ranged in amongst some of the most powerful men and women in the land were local people who didn't have much influence at all. For once politics was a million miles away. What united them was genuine affection for Derek. I got to the end with difficulty though. The telling of the story about the bunch of daffodils, which Derek took to my wife Sarah's bedside when she was dying, eased things a little, but I almost broke down.

On the steps afterwards I stood and talked to Mrs Enright, Derek's much loved mother. "I have never spoken insincerely at any funeral", I said, "but obviously there are some where you have to tread carefully and pick your words, dwelling on some things but not on others. Today I have had no problems for this in many ways was an easy one to speak at. I could tell the total truth. Derek was a kind and brave man".

Geoff Lofthouse

On the day after her birth, while still in the Special Care Baby Unit in the John Radcliffe Hospital in Oxford, our daughter Katy lay wired to many monitors and drug lines because of her difficult birth, during which she had been asphyxiated. Her grandparents all rushed to Oxford to see Katy and to support us. As soon as Derek saw his first grandchild he was transfixed: "The prettiest Kate in Christendom" was his verdict. The comparison with Kate from "The Taming of the Shrew" was appropriate: she was, and is still, a spirited little girl. We all agreed that life might be calmer with a Bianca, but a lot less fun.

Two months later, we were sitting together in hospital again. This time it was St Thomas' Hospital in Westminster. It was just two weeks before he died and he was admiring pictures of her Christening. Katy had reached the ripe old age of nine weeks, but was now strong and healthy. He held her and talked to her with great tenderness and love. Derek always had a song ready and was soon crooning "Bye Baby Bunting" to her as she gazed into his face.

The two met each other only in hospitals, but Katy will be able to grow up knowing all about her remarkable grandpa. We're planning to take her to see "The Taming of the Shrew" one day, too....

Sally-Ann Enright

I have lots of memories of my father; what he was like and what he did for me and others. Initially, though, it is difficult to think of my dad without thinking of his 11th floor hospital room with the stunning view of the House of Commons. He was very thin ill and dying. It makes me sad to think of him there.

I don't want to forget that last short time. I was there when I could be. We didn't talk about anything very serious. We watched the telly. I told him what I'd been doing at work and fell off the corner of his blow up mattress. I didn't tell him that I loved him any more than the usual, on greeting and leaving. I was thinking it and he knew. But although I will never forget that room that is not how I will remember him.

What will come to mind is his shouts of "Come on Enright" in his deep booming voice, as he watched me play rugby from the touchline. I will remember him sneaking into the lavvy to play his electronic bridge game without my mother knowing – but Dad, she always knew. There was the evening he turned down the plushiest accommodation Newcastle had to offer to be with me in my dive of a hotel.

Nor will I forget the way I could tease him about his hair, "Well the one on the left is fine Dad, but the one on the right is out of place."

The one memory which will link the time in the hospital with all the others however is his stock phrase. It was with these words that he used to greet every failure to get his own way with the family. He only used them once in the hospital and, as always, they were said with a smile and a twinkle in his eye.

"It's only me" he said in a mournful tone as if he thought we didn't care. But we did and you always knew that didn't you Dad?

Simon Enright

It's very strange the things that spring to mind when you look back at a lifetime of memories. Towards the end of his life one thing that saddened me was that my father would not be around to play with my children, his grandchildren. What will I tell them?

When I was asked to think of memories of my father I was surprised at the things that stuck in my mind. I was never very gifted when it came to remembering things so it's strange what things stand out.

When the four of us were very young we would always have a birthday party, at which we would invite all of our friends. It was always a very exciting day that was packed with party food and party games and must have been exhausting for the adults involved, who had to organise and supervise the whole affair.

I always remember my father being the life and soul of the party, keeping numerous children from the ages of two to twelve all happy, excited, squealing and screaming for hours. He was wonderful. We would creep up behind him as he climbed the stone spiral staircase of our Victorian house. "What time is it Mr Wolf", we would chant, waiting for him to turn around and catch one of us when it was "Mr Wolf's dinner time".

We could have played for hours, but, inevitably, due to complete over excitement someone would fall over on those huge stairs. But my father was always there to blow away all the pain and stem the flow of tears. Everyone appreciated his skill at keeping the party going, even at times of minor distress. That was one of his many talents.

Holidays were always fun for the Enrights, whether we were camping in the rain in the Yorkshire Dales or sunning ourselves by the pool in some Mediterranean country.

From as far back as I can remember, until early teens, we would go on holiday with the Grundy's, our great family friends. They too had four children, all similar in age to us.

One year we decided to go to Llandogo, a small village in Wales. We stayed on a campsite which was sited right next to the river, in the height of the summer season. We had been there before and made a few friends with the locals, the farmer's dog and other campsite residents. But that was not to be repeated this year.

My father drove for many hours from Pontefract to Llandogo, in our old yellow Toyota, with tent in tow and four children, who at varying intervals had to get out because they felt sick, had to buy sweets or just generally swap positions – who would get to sit in the boot of the estate car?! He was always very patient and uncomplaining. What made this particular trip all the more difficult was that our Boxer dog, Polly, had just had five puppies. They came with us as they were too young to leave their mother. We arrived at the campsite, met the Grundy's, pitched our tent and fed the six dogs.

For my father it was one of the most relaxing holidays ever. What with eight kids and six dogs, everyone could find something to do and keep each other amused. It gave him the chance to have a pint in the pub with Mr Grundy while we all got on with the business of playing, swimming, and eating.

I guess it wasn't at all strange to us that not a sole person wanted to pitch their tent anywhere near ours. The eighteen members of our party were left to their own devices. Funny that!

Jackie Enright

The one thing I will always be able to treasure is that my father was able to give me away at my wedding. His own father died young and so he had also been honoured by standing up for his two sisters. On my wedding day I remember waking up early with the excitement and going downstairs only to greet Dad who had a breakfast tray in his hands. His surprise was acute that I had managed to get up at 8.00am. I'm known in the family for not being very good at getting up.

Just before going into the wedding car Dad asked me if I was happy and ready to get married. "Of course I'm happy," I said, more worried about making it to the car without his footmarks on my dress. Then again, just before he walked me down the aisle he said, "I can call it off now. Nothing matters as long as you are going to be happy." I told him I was and with that he was happy to give me away.

As always, even though he was the most practised of speakers, he was nervous when it came to the reception. He needn't have worried. It was a super speech. There are two jokes I still remember. "So at last I can now call you Mandy Dandy," he said and also, "I don't believe I'm losing a daughter so much as getting rid of all her stuff."

He paid for us to have the first night of our honeymoon at Monk Fryston Hall. He quipped before we went, "I'm paying for the meal when you get there as long as you don't order too much champagne." I think he got a pleasant surprise as John and I only wanted a bowl of soup and a bottle of wine.

When I went to visit him during his last days, it was the same question that he asked, "Are you happy Mandy?" he said. "Yes Dad," I replied, "Thank you."

Mandy Dandy

In May 1974 Featherstone Rovers reached the final of the Challenge Cup. As they did later in 1983, the population of the village jumped on board coaches and headed down to Wembley for the event. Their opponents were the mighty Bradford Northern, runaway favourites for the Cup. But around our area we all knew something that the rest of the world didn't: Fev were going to win. We were sure because Fev had Vince Farrar and John Newlove and the rest, a team of Colliers which included our dustbin men. Unstoppable.

Daddy managed to get hold of two tickets. We didn't know or ask how. At the proud age of 9, I had the chance, along with my father at the age of 38, of going to the greatest sporting event either of our generations would ever witness. Unfortunately I had also entered various speaking competitions at the Pontefract Music Festival, which took place on the morning of the Final. I was determined, although when it came to it I was terrified, to take part in the Festival.

Without so much as a murmur (at least in front of me) my father gave up the tickets to let me take part in the Festival. It was a huge piece of luck that I won a medal for winning the "Under 12 Reading at Sight" class, even though I had been too scared even to stand up during the "Verse Reading" competition. It was also incredibly lucky to be a neighbour of the Blazas, who very kindly invited us to their house to watch the Final live on TV that afternoon in colour, the very first time we had seen colour TV. Fev won and we shouted like anything.

What a sacrifice, though, on my father's behalf. Every child remembers some trivial moment in their parents' lives for which they are ever grateful. My father gave up a seat at Wembley for Fev's greatest victory, because I was taking part in a little speaking competition. I will never forget it.

Duncan Enright

Recently he sent me a card on Mother's Day that read 'To Mummy from her little boy' and which carried the verse:

This clever duck has come along to sing a song of joy
And wish you Happy Mother's Day from me, your little boy
With lots of love.

To which he added:

If you insist on a Mother's Day card
You must take the rhyme from this bloody silly bard!

Helen Enright

Our honeymoon to Greece was a joyous affair, much in the style of Cliff Richard's Summer Holiday film. It was an all singing and all dancing time! We set off being driven by Father Fooks, the priest who had married us, in a beat up Dormobile. In the back were also six boys from the John Fisher school together with my bridesmaid, Dru Yeo, and two old boys Michael Weston and Peter Humfrey – who years later was to conduct Derek's funeral service in Westminster Cathedral, a full fledged Canon of the Church of Rome.

The Dormobile had been a mistake from the start, but we were beguiled by the price. "If you can bring it back in one piece you can have it at the cost of the petrol," said the Fisher parent who owned the garage, laughingly, never dreaming his offer would be taken up. With infinite care the Dormobile was nursed through each day and it climbed, grumbling, slithering and emitting black smoke. We went up the Alps not once but twice. In Greece it became so unbearably hot that we had to remove all the windows, risking exhaust fumes rather than suffocation.

Like all good Catholics, however, it saw Rome and died – nearly. For two days it hovered precariously on the brink of being written off to experience as we shouldered the bags. But somehow the boys and Father Fooks teased life back into the choking engine and after spending much of our hard earned funds, the Odyssey continued.

Our adventures in Greece are too numerous to mention but we spent sunburned days travelling on and then resting in, at that time, little known places. We drank deeply of the local wine and gorged on the olive oil cooked food. We swam in phosphorescent seas and talked and sang endlessly in the Olive groves.

Sadly two of the party that set out are now dead – Derek's death makes the third. No doubt we shall merrily meet in Heaven – we'll know instantly that we're there because we visited that long ago summer in 1963.

Jane Enright